The Comprehensive US Error Coins Handbook:

Expert Insights and Detailed Visuals to Identify Hidden Treasures and Maximize Your Collection's Value

Thomas Reed

TABLE OF CONTENTS

Introduction

Brief Overview of U.S. Error Coins and Their Significance

Imagine finding a coin that looks different from the rest. Maybe it's a penny that's missing part of its design, or a quarter that has an extra layer of metal. These aren't just oddities; they are treasures with stories to tell. Welcome to the fascinating world of U.S. error coins.

Error coins are like hidden gems within the vast landscape of numismatics, the study and collection of coins. Unlike standard coins, which are produced to be uniform and flawless, error coins bear unique characteristics due to mistakes during their creation. These errors can range from simple misalignments to striking anomalies that result in entirely unique designs. Each error coin is a testament to the complexities and occasional mishaps of the minting process.

The significance of U.S. error coins extends far beyond their quirky appearances. For collectors, these coins are prized for their rarity and the intriguing glimpses they offer into the world of minting. They reveal the delicate balance between precision and error in coin production, and they highlight moments in history when things didn't go exactly as planned. Collecting error coins isn't just about owning a piece of metal; it's about holding a piece of history, a tangible connection to the past.

Some error coins, like the famous 1955 doubled die cent or the 2000 Sacagawea dollar mule error, have become legendary within the numismatic community. Their stories of discovery and the subsequent buzz they generated add layers of excitement and value. These coins can command high prices, making them not only fascinating but also potentially lucrative finds.

But it's not just the monetary value that attracts collectors. There's a certain thrill in the hunt for error coins, whether you're sorting through pocket change or examining a dealer's inventory. Each discovery is a small victory, a testament to your keen eye and understanding of the minting process. This hobby encourages a deeper appreciation for the artistry and craftsmanship involved in coin production.

Error coins often tell the untold stories of the minting process's human and mechanical aspects. Every error coin you come across has its unique journey of how it came to be. For instance, the 1943 bronze cent was a result of a few bronze planchets being left in the presses as the Mint switched to steel to conserve copper for the war effort. This switch and the subsequent errors give us a peek into the country's history and the Mint's operations during wartime.

Collecting error coins is a hobby that combines the joy of discovery with a deep appreciation for history. Each coin is a physical artifact from a specific moment in time, offering insights into the technology, economics, and artistry of its era. For example, the 1974-D aluminum cent was part of an experiment to reduce production costs, and its rarity today speaks volumes about the trials and decisions faced by the Mint.

Moreover, error coins can serve as conversation starters and educational tools. They can spark interest in young collectors or casual observers, leading to a broader appreciation for numismatics. Sharing the story of a unique coin you've found can be a gateway for others to learn about history, economics, and even the science of metallurgy. The thrill of finding an error coin in your pocket change or at a flea market can ignite a lifelong passion for coin collecting.

This book is your guide to the captivating world of U.S. error coins. It aims to uncover the stories behind these mistakes, providing you with historical context, expert insights, and practical advice. Whether you're a seasoned collector or just beginning your numismatic journey, you'll find something to inspire and inform you within these pages.

Explanation of the Book's Unique Approach and Structure

This book is not just another numismatic guide. It's a journey through time, a collection of tales that bring the world of error coins to life in a way that's both informative and entertaining. Our approach is to blend the technical details of coin errors with the rich narratives of their histories and the people who discovered them.

The structure of this book is designed to take you on a comprehensive journey, each chapter building on the last to deepen your understanding and appreciation of error coins.

Chapter 1: The Birth of Error Coins

We start at the beginning, with an introduction to the minting process. Here, you'll learn how coins are made and, crucially, how things can go wrong. From planchet errors to die errors, this chapter covers the various types of mistakes that can occur. We'll also look at some historical milestones in error coin discoveries, setting the stage for the stories to come.

Understanding how coins are made is crucial to appreciating how errors occur. This foundational knowledge sets the stage for recognizing and valuing error coins, as you will learn about the various stages where things can go awry, leading to the creation of these unique collectibles.

Chapter 2: Detailed Analysis of Specific Error Coins

This chapter takes a closer look at some of the most intriguing and valuable error coins across various denominations. From pennies to dollars, each section provides a comprehensive examination of a notable error coin, detailing its unique characteristics, historical context, and impact on the numismatic market. By understanding these specific examples, you'll gain a deeper appreciation of how errors can occur and why they are so highly prized by collectors.

Chapter 3: Hidden Histories

This chapter delves into the fascinating tales behind specific error coins. You'll read about the historical events and minting circumstances that led to these errors. Each story is a blend of fact and personal anecdote, bringing the coins to life in a way that lists and descriptions alone cannot. Imagine learning about a coin discovered during a time of national crisis or one that slipped through quality control during a period of rapid technological change.

By exploring the specific circumstances and stories behind notable error coins, this chapter humanizes the minting process and highlights the serendipity involved in their creation. You will read about the people who discovered these coins and how their finds have impacted the numismatic world.

Chapter 4: Expert Insights

In this chapter, we turn to the experts. Through interviews with numismatists, mint employees, and seasoned collectors, we gather a wealth of knowledge and advice. These insights will help you identify and value error coins, providing practical tips that you can apply in your own collecting efforts. Hearing directly from those immersed in the world of error coins adds depth and authenticity to our exploration.

Their insights provide valuable lessons on identifying, authenticating, and valuing error coins. These expert opinions add depth to your understanding and equip you with the knowledge needed to become proficient in this niche area of coin collecting.

Chapter 5: Practical Collecting Guide

Whether you're a novice or a seasoned collector, this chapter offers practical advice to help you navigate the world of error coins. From step-by-step tutorials on how to search for and authenticate error coins, to tips on preserving your finds, this guide is packed with useful information. We'll also discuss market trends and investment strategies, helping you make informed decisions about your collection.

From step-by-step tutorials on how to search for and authenticate error coins, to tips on preserving your finds, this guide is packed with useful information. We'll also discuss market trends and investment strategies, helping you make informed decisions about your collection.

Chapter 6: Mastering Numismatics Through Self-Assessment and Interactive Learning

This chapter provides a structured approach for enhancing numismatic skills through self-assessment and interactive exercises. It includes visual comparison challenges, market analysis simulations, and practical valuation exercises to improve error detection and coin valuation skills. Additionally, it emphasizes building a historical context repository and implementing feedback loops, such as journaling and peer reviews, to support continuous learning and engagement with the numismatic community.

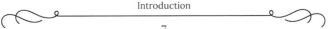

Chapter 7: Comprehensive Reference Section

The final chapter serves as a detailed reference guide. Here, you'll find a catalog of U.S. error coins by denomination, complete with high-quality images, descriptions, rarity scales, and current market values. We've also included a glossary of numismatic terms and a detailed index, making it easy to find specific information.

With detailed catalogs, high-quality images, and up-to-date market values, this chapter is a valuable resource for any collector. The glossary and index ensure that you can easily navigate the book and find the information you need.

Chapter 8: Documenting and Cataloging Your Collection

Effective documentation and cataloging are vital for managing a coin collection. This chapter provides a comprehensive guide on creating a digital catalog and includes essential information to record about each coin. We also cover best practices for organizing and maintaining your collection.

Creating a Digital Catalog: Learn how to use software and online tools to create a detailed digital catalog of your collection. This section covers selecting the right tools, setting up your catalog, and ensuring it is both user-friendly and comprehensive.

Essential Information to Include in Your Records: Understand what information is crucial to record for each coin, including mint details, error types, provenance, and condition. This helps in tracking the history and value of your collection accurately.

Best Practices for Organizing and Maintaining Your Collection: Discover the best practices for keeping your collection organized and well-maintained. This includes storage solutions, regular updates to your catalog, and measures to protect your coins from damage and theft.

By combining historical narratives, expert advice, practical guides, and interactive content, this book offers a fresh and engaging perspective on U.S. error coins. This is not just a catalog of errors; it's a celebration of the stories and people behind these fascinating coins. Whether you are a seasoned collector or a curious newcomer, you'll find this book an invaluable resource and a captivating read.

The Birth of Error Coins

Introduction to the Minting Process

The journey of a coin from a simple piece of metal to a finely crafted currency is a fascinating blend of art and science. The minting process, often overlooked by many, is a complex ballet of heavy machinery, precise engineering, and careful craftsmanship that results in the coins jingling in your pocket. Let's explore this intricate world to better understand how errors, those delightful quirks in the numismatic universe, come into being.

The Basics of Coin Minting

At its core, minting involves converting metal sheets into coins. This transformation occurs in several stages: blanking, annealing, striking, and inspection. Initially, large rolls of metal are fed into blanking presses where thousands of coin-shaped pieces, known as blanks or planchets, are punched out. These blanks are then annealed in large furnaces to soften them, making them ready for striking.

The real magic happens in the coining press, where these blanks are struck between two dies. The upper and lower dies impress the design onto the blank, creating the coin's obverse (front) and reverse (back) faces. This is done under immense pressure, ensuring that every detail of the intricate designs is perfectly transferred.

The Role of Quality Control

Even in modern mints, where automation dominates, quality control is paramount. After striking, coins are subjected to a series of checks to ensure they meet the mint's stringent standards. Coins are examined for correct dimensions, composition, and clarity of design. Those that don't pass muster are melted down and recycled, ready to start the process anew.

Despite these rigorous checks, errors can and do occur. The complexity of the minting process, combined with the sheer volume of coins produced, makes it inevitable that some errors slip through, much to the delight of collectors.

How Errors Enhance the Minting Narrative

Error coins are more than just manufacturing mishaps; they are a testament to the minting process's complexity and precision. Each error tells a story—a snapshot of a moment when the machinery of currency production faltered, however slightly. For those passionate about numismatics, these errors provide a deeper insight into the otherwise hidden world of coin minting, offering a tangible connection to the otherwise mechanical and impersonal process.

The very act of minting, which involves numerous meticulous steps and the coordination of advanced machinery and skilled labor, is prone to a myriad of small anomalies. From the mixing of the metal alloys used in the planchets to the final inspection and distribution, each phase holds potential pitfalls that can lead to the creation of an error coin. Understanding this complex dance gives numismatists and enthusiasts alike a greater appreciation for each coin in their collection, especially those that defy the norm.

Further Exploration of Coin Production Techniques

To truly grasp the intricacies of coin minting, one must consider the finer details of each step in the process. For instance, the blanking phase not only involves cutting out the coin shapes but also includes the careful selection and treatment of the metal alloys. These metals must possess certain qualities to ensure durability and the ability to clearly depict intricate designs.

The Annealing Process

After blanking, the annealing process, a critical yet underappreciated stage, involves heating the coin blanks to a specific temperature to soften the metal. This step is crucial for preparing the metal for striking by making it pliable enough to take on the designs without cracking. The precise control of temperature and timing in the annealing ovens can significantly impact the quality of the final coin.

Striking: The Moment of Creation

The striking stage is where the true transformation occurs. It is here that the coin receives its identity and value. The pressure applied during this process must be meticulously calibrated. Too much pressure and the coin can split; too little, and the design will not be fully formed. The dies used in this process are works of art themselves, crafted by skilled engravers who can spend hundreds of hours designing and refining a single coin die.

Quality Control: The Final Guard

Following the striking of the coin, quality control acts as the final safeguard against errors. However, this stage can also introduce errors if not properly managed. Technicians must be highly trained to spot even the slightest deviations in a coin's appearance, which might indicate an error. This careful inspection ensures that only coins meeting the highest standards reach circulation.

Thus, the minting process is akin to a well-orchestrated symphony, where each movement must be performed with precision and grace. However, just as in any performance, slight missteps can occur, resulting in the fascinating error coins that captivate collectors and numismatists. Each error coin not only serves as a reminder of the complexities inherent in the minting process but also enriches the tapestry of numismatic collection, offering insights and stories that continue to fascinate and educate.

Common Types of Errors

In the world of coin collecting, error coins are like the misprinted stamps of the numismatic world: rare, intriguing, and highly sought after. Understanding the different types of errors can help collectors identify potential treasures in their change. Let's explore some of the most common errors that occur during the minting process, offering a window into the precision and complexity of coin production.

Planchet Errors

Before a coin is struck, the blank itself might have issues. Planchet errors can occur when the metal sheet used to create the blanks has impurities or when the blanking press misfires. Common planchet errors include clips, where part of the coin is missing due to the blank being cut improperly. This usually happens when the blanking machine punches overlapping holes in the metal strip, leading to irregularly shaped planchets that result in clipped coins.

Laminations are another type of planchet error where parts of the coin flake off due to impurities in the metal or poor mixing of the alloy. These errors can give coins a peeled, blistered appearance, particularly if the lamination affects large areas of the coin's surface. Sometimes, small fissures can be seen before the lamination actually peels away, providing tell-tale signs of this defect.

Die Errors

The dies that strike the coin can also be a source of errors. If a die is damaged, improperly made, or wears out, it can produce errors on every coin it strikes until it is replaced. One common die error is the doubled die, where the elements of the coin's design appear doubled. This occurs during the die-making process, when shifts or misalignments happen as the die receives multiple impressions from a hub that imprints the design.

Die cracks are another prevalent error, leading to raised lines on the coin. These cracks can occur when a die becomes fatigued and develops small fissures. As the die continues to be used, these fissures can grow, creating raised lines that appear as part of the coin's design. Cuds, on the other hand, occur when a piece of the die breaks off completely. The resulting coins show a raised, unstruck area where the broken part of the die was located, often creating a distinctive feature that is quite collectible.

Striking Errors

Sometimes, errors occur during the striking process itself. These can be some of the most visually dramatic errors. Misstrikes, for example, occur when the coin is not aligned correctly when struck. This can result in off-center coins, where part of the design is missing, or in extreme cases, only part of the design is struck on the planchet. These errors create a unique aesthetic, sometimes enhancing the coin's value significantly, especially if the misstrike is particularly severe.

Double denomination errors occur when a planchet intended for one denomination is accidentally fed into a press set up for another denomination. For example, a dime planchet in a quarter press results in a coin that has the size and metal composition of a dime but the design of a quarter. This type of error is fascinating because it blends characteristics from two different coins, making them highly prized by collectors.

Another striking error is the broadstrike, which happens when a coin is struck without the collar that normally holds the coin in place during the striking process. Without the collar, the metal flows outward, resulting in a coin that is larger and misshapen. These coins often have a smooth, stretched appearance as the design spreads beyond the normal boundaries.

The Impact of Errors on Numismatics

Each type of error tells a story about what might have gone wrong in the minting process. For collectors, these errors not only add a unique piece to their collection but also serve as a fascinating glimpse into the art and science of minting. Errors are not merely flaws but windows into the mechanical soul of the minting machinery, reflecting the high stakes and intricacies involved in the art of coining.

Error coins, therefore, are more than just numismatic curiosities—they are teaching tools and historical documents. They highlight the mint's constant battle between maintaining high standards and the realities of mass production. Each error coin is a snapshot of a moment when the usual precision faltered, offering collectors a story and a mystery to unravel.

Collecting error coins is not only about seeking rarity or investment; it's about pursuing the stories behind the coins, the unscripted moments of minting. These coins remind us that even in a process defined by precision, unpredictability is a hidden architect, making each error coin a unique piece of numismatic art.

Historical Overview of Notable Error Coin Discoveries

The history of coin collecting is peppered with the discovery of error coins, each bringing its own tale of surprise, excitement, and sometimes, significant financial reward. These discoveries often become the stuff of legend within the numismatic community, celebrated for their rarity and the stories behind their creation.

The 1955 Doubled Die Lincoln Cent

One of the most famous error coins is the 1955 doubled die Lincoln cent. The error occurred when the die used to strike the coins was misaligned during a second impression. This resulted in a coin with doubled features, most noticeably in the date and inscriptions. Discovered soon after their release, these coins sparked a frenzy among collectors and remain highly sought after today. The dramatic nature of the doubling, easily visible to the naked eye, makes these coins particularly appealing to both novice and experienced collectors.

The 2000 Sacagawea Dollar Mule

In 2000, a remarkable error occurred when a Sacagawea dollar reverse die was paired with a state quarter obverse die. This "mule" coin, featuring two different denominations, was accidentally released into circulation. It was not discovered until 2000 by a collector in Arkansas, making it an instant numismatic celebrity due to its unusual error and rarity. This coin's accidental fusion of two different denominational designs captures the imagination and symbolizes the unpredictability and charm of error coin collecting.

Recent Discoveries

The hunt for error coins continues in the modern day, with new errors being discovered as more people take up coin collecting. With the rise of internet forums and social media, sharing knowledge about these rare finds has become easier, increasing the number of people on the lookout for these collectible anomalies. Recent discoveries include various misstrikes and off-center coins found in circulation, often by eagle-eyed individuals who carefully examine their change.

The 1943 Copper Penny

Among the most coveted error coins is the 1943 copper penny. During World War II, copper was crucial for war materials, leading the U.S. Mint to switch penny production from copper to steel. However, a few copper planchets from 1942 were mistakenly left in the presses and struck with the 1943 date. These rare coins are highly prized today, with one selling for over $200,000 at auction. The story of their discovery and the historical context of their creation add layers of depth to their allure.

The Kansas State Quarter "Humpback Bison"

A notable recent error involved the Kansas state quarter, where an error in the die created an image of a bison with a pronounced hump, leading collectors to nickname it the "Humpback Bison." This quirky variation was quickly noticed and gained popularity for its odd appearance, sparking interest among collectors looking for unusual pieces to add to their collections.

Broader Impact of Error Coins on Numismatics

Error coins serve as a reminder of the ever-present human element in the mechanized process of coin production. They connect collectors not just to history but to the stories of those who mint and collect coins, adding a layer of human interest to each piece. Whether discovered in pocket change or through deliberate searching, each error coin discovery adds a new chapter to the rich history of numismatics, bridging the gap between past and present, and between collectors across generations.

These coins not only fascinate due to their rarity or the mistakes they embody but also because they challenge our understanding of how coins are supposed to look and function. Each error tells a unique story, from minor quirks to major blunders, offering insights into the technological, human, and sometimes surprisingly random aspects of minting.

Error coins illuminate the intricacies of the minting process, showcasing what happens when things go awry. They remind us that perfection is a target, not always achievable, and that mistakes—whether in coin minting or in life—can sometimes result in unexpected treasures. For collectors, these errors transform ordinary coin collecting into a treasure hunt, each find providing a thrilling story of chance and discovery. As we continue to uncover and cherish these mistakes, the world of numismatics grows richer, fueled by a community that values and celebrates the wonderfully imperfect.

Detailed Analysis of Specific Error Coins

In this chapter, we delve deeply into some of the most intriguing and valuable error coins in numismatics, covering various denominations from pennies to dollars. Each section provides a detailed description of the coin, its historical context, and its rarity and market value. These error coins not only offer a window into the minting process but also illustrate how such anomalies can create significant numismatic interest and value.

Disclaimer

Due to the rarity of many of the coins covered in this book, acquiring images of each piece was a significant challenge, as many are held in private collections. We have made every effort to provide a valuable resource by including detailed videos of the coin errors whenever available. Where specific images were unavailable, we have instead provided information and resources to guide readers towards a deeper understanding of various error coins. This approach is intended to aid collectors in developing a keen eye for distinguishing these unique characteristics, fostering both knowledge and appreciation of this fascinating area of numismatics.

Penny Errors

1955
Doubled Die Lincoln Cent

Detailed Description:

The 1955 Doubled Die Lincoln Cent is one of the most famous error coins in American numismatics. This error is characterized by noticeable doubling on the date and inscriptions, making the digits and letters appear blurry. This doubling occurs during the die-making process when the die receives multiple, misaligned impressions.

Historical Context:

This particular error was made at a time when quality control measures at the U.S. Mint were less stringent than today, allowing several thousand doubled die coins to enter circulation. The discovery of these coins sparked significant public interest in coin collecting during the mid-20th century.

Rarity and Market Value:

Although thousands of these coins were originally circulated, they are now considered quite rare. A 1955 Doubled Die Lincoln Cent can sell for anywhere from $1,000 to over $20,000, depending on its condition.

1972
Doubled Die Obverse
Lincoln Cent

Detailed Description:

Another striking error, the 1972 Doubled Die Obverse features prominent doubling on the coin's obverse side, affecting the date and inscriptions significantly. Unlike the 1955 error, this doubling is more pronounced and easier to identify without magnification.

Historical Context:

The error resulted from a similar mishap in the die hubbing process as the 1955 coin. It was discovered shortly after its release and quickly became a collector's item due to the dramatic nature of the misprint.

Rarity and Market Value:

It is slightly more common than the 1955 doubled die but still commands high prices in the market. Prices range from $500 for coins in lower grades to over $5,000 for those in pristine condition.

1983
Doubled Die Reverse
Lincoln Cent

Detailed Description:

The 1983 Doubled Die Reverse features doubling on the reverse side, particularly around the phrase "ONE CENT" and the lower United States of America. This double impression gives the text and design elements a shadowed appearance.

Historical Context:

Coming into circulation in the early 1980s, this coin exemplifies the ongoing issues with die production that have periodically surfaced at the U.S. Mint. Its discovery helped to further energize modern coin collecting.

Rarity and Market Value:

As with other doubled die errors, the 1983 reversed version is sought after by collectors. These coins are typically valued between $250 and $3,000, heavily dependent on their condition.

1922
No D Strong Reverse Lincoln Cent

Detailed Description:

This rare variety of the 1922 Lincoln Cent features no visible "D" mintmark despite being produced at the Denver Mint. This specific error is characterized by a strong reverse with sharp details, distinguishing it from other 'no D' varieties which typically have weak reverses.

Historical Context:

The absence of the mintmark is due to overpolishing of the die. In 1922, the Denver mint was the only one to produce Lincoln Cents, making this "no D" version especially peculiar and noteworthy. It is one of the most famous and sought-after varieties among Lincoln Cents.

Rarity and Market Value:

Very few examples of the 1922 No D Strong Reverse exist in higher grades, making them exceptionally valuable. Prices can range from $500 in lower conditions to over $10,000 for well-preserved pieces.

1943
Copper Lincoln Cent

Detailed Description:

In 1943, due to wartime metal conservation, Lincoln Cents were made from zinc-coated steel. However, a few were mistakenly struck on leftover copper planchets from 1942. These copper coins from 1943 are some of the most coveted error coins in U.S. numismatics.

Historical Context:

The 1943 copper pennies are accidents arising from the transitional period in minting materials. Their existence was not confirmed by the U.S. Mint, adding to their mystery and desirability among collectors.

Rarity and Market Value:

As one of the most famous error coins, a genuine 1943 copper cent can fetch well over $100,000, depending on its condition and provenance, with particularly fine specimens reaching into the several hundreds of thousands.

1995
Doubled Die Obverse
Lincoln Cent

Detailed Description:

The 1995 Doubled Die Obverse features noticeable doubling on the obverse side of the coin, particularly around Lincoln's portrait and the inscriptions "LIBERTY" and "IN GOD WE TRUST." The doubling is especially prominent and can be seen with the naked eye.

Historical Context:

Discovered while still in circulation, the 1995 doubled die brought renewed public attention to coin collecting. Its occurrence during a time of robust collecting activity helped make this one of the more frequently encountered and recognized doubled dies.

Rarity and Market Value:

Though not as rare as earlier doubled die errors, the 1995 doubled die cent remains popular. It typically commands prices ranging from $20 for circulated examples to several hundred dollars for coins in mint condition.

1984
Doubled Ear Lincoln Cent

Detailed Description:

This error features a doubling of Lincoln's ear, giving the appearance that he has an extra earlobe. This specific doubling is unique to the 1984 Lincoln cent and is a result of a class IV doubling, or "offset hub doubling."

Historical Context:

The error was caused by a misalignment during the hubbing process and was quickly caught by numismatists who specialize in die varieties. Its distinctive appearance makes it easily identifiable and a favorite among collectors of modern error coins.

Rarity and Market Value:

he 1984 Doubled Ear Lincoln Cent is moderately rare. Collectors may pay between $50 for lower grades to over $250 for uncirculated examples.

Nickel Errors

1939

Doubled Monticello Jefferson Nickel

Detailed Description:

This coin features doubling on the Monticello building and the word "Monticello" itself. The doubling is most evident on the façade of Monticello, giving it a doubled architectural appearance.

Historical Context:

The Jefferson Nickel series had just begun six years earlier, in 1938. This specific error brought a lot of attention to the new series, enhancing its popularity among collectors.

Rarity and Market Value:

While not as rare as some of the famed penny errors, the 1939 Doubled Monticello nickel holds considerable value, generally ranging from $100 to several thousand dollars for top-grade specimens.

1942-P
Over S Jefferson Nickel

Detailed Description:

This wartime nickel from 1942 features a unique error where an "S" mintmark was initially stamped on the die, but was later overpunched with a "P" mintmark. The resulting coin shows both letters, with the "S" visible beneath the "P."

Historical Context:

1942 was a significant year as the U.S. Mint began using a silver alloy for nickels due to nickel being a critical war material. The overpunch error occurred during a hectic period of adjustments in mint operations.

Rarity and Market Value:

The 1942-P Over S Jefferson Nickel is a wartime curiosity that is quite rare and valuable, fetching anywhere from $300 to over $4,000 in uncirculated condition.

1943/2-P
Jefferson Nickel

Detailed Description:

This intriguing error coin features an overdate where a 1943 die was struck over a 1942 die. The numeral "2" is visible beneath the "3," making it a clear example of an overdate error. This type of error occurs when old dies are reused and not properly re-engraved.

Historical Context:

During World War II, the U.S. Mint was under pressure to produce vast amounts of coinage, sometimes leading to hasty or improper retooling of dies. The 1943/2 overdate error reflects the challenging conditions and resource constraints during the war.

Rarity and Market Value:

The 1943/2-P Jefferson Nickel is a sought-after coin among collectors of wartime mintages and error coins. It typically commands prices ranging from $100 in lower grades to over $2,000 in uncirculated condition.

1945-P
Jefferson Nickel Doubled Die Reverse

Detailed Description:

The 1945-P Doubled Die Reverse Jefferson Nickel displays prominent doubling on the reverse side, particularly around the Monticello building and the denomination "FIVE CENTS." This doubling makes the architectural features of Monticello appear thicker and more defined.

Historical Context:

Struck at the end of World War II, this error coin came from a batch where quality control was still recovering from wartime disruptions. It is one of the more noticeable doubled die errors for nickels from this era.

Rarity and Market Value:

This nickel, due to its clear doubling and historical significance, is relatively rare and can be quite valuable, with prices generally ranging from $200 to $1,500 depending on the grade and the visibility of the doubling.

1949-D
Over S Jefferson Nickel

Detailed Description:

This error features a Denver ("D") mintmark over an initial San Francisco ("S") mintmark. The overmintmark is a result of a die having been first marked for use at the San Francisco mint and then repunched with a "D" for Denver.

Historical Context:

The 1949-D Over S error reflects the period's common practice of reusing and modifying dies between mints to manage production demands efficiently. It is a fascinating example of mint operation logistics.

Rarity and Market Value:

The 1949-D Over S Jefferson Nickel appeals to collectors due to its unique mintmark error. It usually fetches between $30 for circulated examples to around $600 for top-grade coins.

1954-S
Over D Jefferson Nickel

Detailed Description:

In this mintmark error, a San Francisco ("S") mintmark is stamped over a Denver ("D") mintmark. The layers of the mintmarks are discernible with a good magnifying glass, showing the "S" distinctly over the "D."

Historical Context:

Like the 1949-D Over S, this error resulted from the re-purposing of dies between mints. This specific error gives insight into the practices and perhaps the hurried adjustments in mint operations during the mid-20th century.

Rarity and Market Value:

This type of mintmark error is particularly popular among collectors who appreciate mintmark varieties. The 1954-S Over D Nickel typically ranges in price from about $10 in lower grades to several hundred dollars in uncirculated condition.

Dime Errors

1968
No S Proof Roosevelt Dime

Detailed Description:

This error coin is a proof without the "S" mintmark, which should have been present to denote its San Francisco origin. The absence of the mintmark makes this coin especially rare since proofs are typically struck with great care and precision.

Historical Context:

The 1968 No S Proof Roosevelt Dime is part of a series of "No S" mintmark errors that occurred sporadically throughout the 20th century. These errors are particularly significant due to their rarity and the circumstances of their production, which are typically characterized by high quality and low mintage figures.

Rarity and Market Value:

As one of the rarest dimes, its value can exceed $20,000 for coins in pristine condition, making it a prized possession for serious collectors.

1982
No P Roosevelt Dime

Detailed Description:

This coin is notable for the absence of the "P" mintmark, which should have indicated its production at the Philadelphia Mint. Its lack makes it an anomaly among modern dimes.

Historical Context:

The error occurred during a routine year of production, making it an unusual mistake given the typically stringent control measures in place by the 1980s. It was not discovered until several coins had already been released into circulation, causing a frenzy among collectors.

Rarity and Market Value:

The 1982 No P Roosevelt Dime can fetch between $50 in circulated condition to over $500 for uncirculated examples, making it a valuable find for collectors.

1970
No S Proof Roosevelt Dime

Detailed Description:

Like the 1968 No S, the 1970 No S Proof Roosevelt Dime lacks the "S" mintmark, which should have been present to denote its San Francisco origin. This lack of mintmark on a proof coin, where mintmarks are used to indicate the coin's source, makes it one of the notable errors in the Roosevelt series.

Historical Context:

The absence of the mintmark on these specific proof coins is an oversight that happened rarely, with the San Francisco Mint usually meticulous in its proof coin production. This error reflects a lapse in the otherwise stringent proofing process and adds to the collectability and intrigue of this series.

Rarity and Market Value:

The 1970 No S Proof Roosevelt Dime is highly sought after by collectors due to its rarity and the peculiarity of its production error. It regularly commands prices ranging from a few hundred to several thousand dollars, depending on its condition.

1975
No S Proof Roosevelt Dime

Detailed Description:

This is yet another instance of a missing "S" mintmark on a proof coin. The 1975 No S Proof is particularly rare and significant among the Roosevelt dimes, marking it as one of the most coveted error coins in modern numismatics.

Historical Context:

The 1975 No S Proof error is among the rarest of the No S series, with very few examples known to exist. This rarity is partly due to the increased quality control measures that were typically in place during the mid-1970s, making such errors exceedingly unusual.

Rarity and Market Value:

As one of the rarest of the Roosevelt dime errors, the 1975 No S can fetch tens of thousands of dollars in auctions, particularly if in pristine condition. Its rarity and the context of its error make it a centerpiece in many numismatic collections.

1983
No S Proof Roosevelt Dime

Detailed Description:

Continuing the trend in the series, the 1983 No S Proof Roosevelt Dime features the absence of the "S" mintmark on a coin that was intended to be a proof issued by the San Francisco Mint. This error makes the coin highly rare and valuable.

Historical Context:

By the 1980s, the process for creating and checking proof coins had become more automated, yet errors still occurred. The 1983 No S is another example of how even the most technologically advanced processes can fail, adding an interesting chapter to the story of Roosevelt dimes.

Rarity and Market Value:

This dime, while newer than its 1968 and 1970 counterparts, still holds significant value, typically fetching between $300 to $3,000 at auction, with prices varying based on the coin's condition and the market demand at the time of sale.

1942/1
Mercury Dime

Detailed Description:

This overdate error coin, where a 1942 die was struck over a 1941 die, shows parts of the "1" protruding from beneath the "2". This error occurred during the transition between years at the mint and is one of the most famous errors in the Mercury Dime series.

Historical Context:

The early 1940s were a period of hectic production at the U.S. mints, with the pressures of World War II leading to increased and hurried coin production. The 1942/1 Mercury dime is a product of these circumstances and is highly prized both as an error coin and as a historical artifact.

Rarity and Market Value:

The 1942/1 Mercury Dime is a major rarity and highly sought after by both error coin collectors and those specializing in Mercury dimes. Prices can range from a few thousand dollars for lower-grade examples to over $10,000 for specimens in fine condition.

These expanded cases add depth to your exploration of dime errors, showcasing a range of mistakes from missing mintmarks to overdates, reflecting both human error and the complexities of mint operation. Each case provides a snapshot of different eras in coin minting and the evolution of quality control in numismatics.

Quarter Errors

1932-D and 1932-S Washington Quarters

Detailed Description:

Both the 1932-D and 1932-S Washington Quarters are key rarities in the Washington quarter series, with very low mintages making them highly sought after. While not errors per se, their low production numbers and the historical context in which they were minted make them worthy of inclusion in this discussion.

Historical Context:

Minted during the height of the Great Depression, these quarters were produced in limited quantities as the demand for new quarters was low. They represent a significant period in American numismatic history, marked by economic struggle and scarcity.

Rarity and Market Value:

These quarters are extremely valuable due to their scarcity, with values ranging from several hundred dollars in lower grades to over $10,000 in higher grades.

2004-D Extra Leaf Wisconsin State Quarter

Detailed Description:

This error features an additional leaf on the ear of corn on the reverse side of the Wisconsin quarter, which appears as either a "Low Leaf" or "High Leaf" variant. This minor yet distinct variation captures the attention of error coin collectors.

Historical Context:

The State Quarters series was immensely popular, and the discovery of this error added to the excitement and public interest in collecting these coins. The error was likely caused by a die gouge that went unnoticed during production.

Rarity and Market Value:

Depending on the variant and condition, the 2004-D Extra Leaf Wisconsin quarters can bring in anywhere from $200 to over $1,500.

1983-P
Spitting Eagle Washington Quarter

Detailed Description:

This quarter is known for the distinctive die flaw located near the eagle's beak on the reverse side, which resembles the eagle spitting. This visual anomaly is due to a die crack that developed with time and use in the minting process.

Historical Context:

The "Spitting Eagle" variant was discovered and gained popularity among collectors for its quirky appearance. While not a planned part of the design, this error adds character and collectability to the 1983-P Washington Quarter.

Rarity and Market Value:

This error is more of a curiosity than a rarity but is highly sought after by those who collect Washington quarters or error coins in general. It generally fetches modest premiums over face value, ranging from $10 to $100 depending on its condition.

2005-P
Minnesota Doubled Die Quarter

Detailed Description:

This error involves noticeable doubling on the reverse side of the Minnesota state quarter, specifically on the tree line and state outline. The doubling varies from slight to very pronounced, making some variants particularly desirable.

Historical Context:

The Minnesota doubled die quarter is part of the 50 State Quarters series, which saw high public interest and scrutiny from collectors. This specific doubling error is one of several found in the series, reflecting the high production volumes and varying die conditions.

Rarity and Market Value:

The value of these quarters can vary significantly based on the extent of the doubling and overall condition. Prices range from a few dollars for minor errors to over $100 for the most pronounced and desirable doubling errors.

1970-D
Quarter on a 1941 Canadian Quarter

Detailed Description:

This rare error coin was struck using a 1941 Canadian quarter as the planchet. The result is a U.S. quarter that bears residual elements of the Canadian design, including the year, making it an extraordinary error type known as a "foreign planchet error."

Historical Context:

Such errors typically occur when planchets intended for other coinages accidentally end up in the wrong minting batch. This specific error is a fascinating example of how two countries' coinages can become intertwined by mistake.

Rarity and Market Value:

Due to its rarity and the clear visibility of elements from two different national currencies, this error is extremely valuable, with specimens often trading for several thousand dollars depending on the market interest and coin condition.

2007
Wyoming Doubled Die Quarter

Detailed Description:

This quarter from the 50 State series exhibits doubling on the cowboy and horse, the central design elements on the reverse of the Wyoming quarter. The doubling is particularly noticeable on the cowboy's hand and the horse's saddle.

Historical Context:

The error was caused during the minting process, likely due to die degradation or misalignment. It's a sought-after error because it prominently features the primary artistic elements of the quarter.

Rarity and Market Value:

The 2007 Wyoming Doubled Die Quarter attracts premiums from collectors, typically ranging from $20 to several hundred dollars, especially for coins in uncirculated condition or with prominent doubling.

Half Dollar Errors

1964
Kennedy Half Dollar Doubled Die Obverse

Detailed Description:

This coin exhibits clear doubling on the obverse, particularly around President Kennedy's profile and the date. This type of doubling makes the features appear more pronounced and distorted.

Historical Context:

Released shortly after President Kennedy's assassination, the Kennedy Half Dollar quickly became an icon of American numismatics. This error added a layer of desirability and rarity to an already popular coin.

Rarity and Market Value:

The 1964 Kennedy Half Dollar Doubled Die Obverse is a coveted item among collectors of Kennedy memorabilia and error coins alike, often fetching upwards of $1,000 in good condition.

1972-D
No FG Kennedy Half Dollar

Detailed Description:

The "No FG" error refers to the missing initials of the coin's designer, Frank Gasparro, which should appear on the reverse below the eagle. This omission can be attributed to over-polishing of the die.

Historical Context:

This error is among a series of "No FG" errors found in Kennedy Half Dollars. These coins are particularly sought after because they represent a breakdown in the usual attention to detail during the minting process.

Rarity and Market Value:

Coins with the "No FG" error are highly valued, with prices typically ranging from $50 for lower grades to several hundred dollars for pristine examples.

1966
Kennedy Half Dollar
Doubled Die Reverse

Detailed Description:

This error features distinct doubling on the reverse side of the coin, particularly noticeable in the lettering of "UNITED STATES OF AMERICA" and "HALF DOLLAR." The eagle's feathers also show signs of doubling, giving them a more textured and layered appearance.

Historical Context:

The 1966 Kennedy Half Dollar is part of the series minted without mint marks regardless of where they were produced. This particular error is attributed to a misalignment during the die hubbing process, a relatively common source of doubling in coin minting.

Rarity and Market Value:

While not as famous as some obverse doubles, the 1966 doubled die reverse is still highly prized among collectors who specialize in Kennedy Half Dollars. It can fetch anywhere from $50 to over $500 depending on its condition and the prominence of the doubling.

1982
Kennedy Half Dollar No FG

Detailed Description:

Similar to the 1972-D, this 1982 Kennedy Half Dollar lacks the "FG" initials of the designer Frank Gasparro on the reverse, below the right leg of the eagle. The absence is typically due to excessive die polishing, which inadvertently removes finer details from the die.

Historical Context:

The early 1980s saw several issues with quality control in U.S. coin production, with the No FG error being among the more common for Kennedy Half Dollars during this period.

Rarity and Market Value:

This variant is relatively common compared to other No FG errors but still holds significant value to collectors, particularly those completing error sets. Prices generally range from $20 to $100 for examples in varying states of preservation.

2008-D Kennedy Half Dollar Double Die Obverse

Detailed Description:

This error includes pronounced doubling on the obverse, affecting Kennedy's profile and the inscriptions around the border. The doubling gives a shadowed effect to the letters and features, making them appear bold and misaligned.

Historical Context:

By 2008, double die errors were less common due to advancements in minting technology and quality assurance, making this particular error quite notable and a topic of interest among modern coin collectors.

Rarity and Market Value:

As a modern error, the 2008-D Double Die Obverse is sought after by collectors of contemporary coin errors. It generally commands a premium, with values ranging from $100 to several hundred dollars, particularly for specimens showing clear, dramatic doubling.

1974-D Kennedy Half Dollar Double Die Obverse

Detailed Description:

The 1974-D features visible doubling on Kennedy's profile and the date. This double die obverse is particularly valued because the doubling is easily visible to the naked eye, making it a favorite among those who collect error coins without the need for magnification.

Historical Context:

The 1974-D is part of a decade known for various minting inconsistencies and errors. Such features were often missed during the quality control process of the Denver Mint at the time.

Rarity and Market Value:

This coin is moderately rare and can fetch prices ranging from around $25 for lightly circulated examples to over $300 for uncirculated grades.

Dollar Errors

1979-P
Wide Rim (Near Date) Susan B. Anthony Dollar

Detailed Description:

The 1979-P Wide Rim, also known as the "Near Date," features a rim that extends unusually close to the date compared to more common variants. This subtle variation affects the overall appearance of the coin's obverse.

Historical Context:

Introduced in 1979, the Susan B. Anthony Dollar was initially unpopular due to its similarity in size and color to the quarter. However, variations like the Wide Rim have garnered interest among collectors due to their scarcity.

Rarity and Market Value:

The 1979-P Wide Rim variant is considerably rarer than the standard version and can command prices ranging from $30 in circulated condition to several hundred dollars in uncirculated condition.

2000-P
Sacagawea Dollar Mule with State Quarter Obverse

Detailed Description:

This spectacular error features the obverse of a state quarter and the reverse of a Sacagawea dollar. This "mule" coin resulted from dies intended for different coin types being incorrectly paired.

Historical Context:

The error is highly unusual and is one of the few instances of such a mistake in modern U.S. Mint history. It likely occurred during the hectic production schedules when the new Sacagawea dollars were being introduced alongside the popular state quarters.

Rarity and Market Value:

As one of the most dramatic and rarest error coins, a 2000-P Sacagawea Dollar Mule can command prices well into the tens of thousands of dollars, depending on the market and the coin's condition.

1979-D
Susan B. Anthony Dollar
"Filled D"

Detailed Description:

This error involves a "D" mintmark that appears filled due to a buildup of grease or debris in the mintmark cavity of the die. The result is a mintmark that is either partially or fully obscured, giving it a blob-like appearance rather than the distinct "D" shape.

Historical Context:

The 1979 Susan B. Anthony Dollars were among the first issues of this new dollar coin series, intended to replace the larger Eisenhower dollar. The "Filled D" is a common die error resulting from minting operations where maintenance and cleaning were insufficient.

Rarity and Market Value:

While not as rare as other die errors, the 1979-D Filled D Susan B. Anthony Dollar is a collectible variant that attracts a premium over face value, typically ranging from $10 to $50, depending on the visibility of the error and the coin's overall condition.

1999-P
Susan B. Anthony Dollar
"Cracked Die"

Detailed Description:

This error features noticeable cracks on the coin's surface, particularly on the obverse around Susan B. Anthony's portrait. These cracks are caused by the breakdown of the die under stress during the minting process.

Historical Context:

The 1999 release marked the final year of production for the Susan B. Anthony Dollar, which saw a brief resurgence in minting to supplement the demand for dollar coins before the introduction of the Sacagawea dollar. Cracked die errors from this year are part of the last batch of these coins, adding historical significance.

Rarity and Market Value:

Cracked die errors from the 1999 series are relatively uncommon and can attract attention from collectors specializing in modern U.S. coin errors, fetching prices from $20 to several hundred dollars, especially if the cracks are prominent and the coin is otherwise in good condition.

2007
Thomas Jefferson Dollar
"Missing Edge Lettering"

Detailed Description:

This error is characterized by the absence of the inscribed edge lettering that should feature the year of minting, "E PLURIBUS UNUM," and "IN GOD WE TRUST." The error occurred due to the coin passing through the minting process without the final edge lettering being applied.

Historical Context:

Introduced in 2007, the Presidential Dollar series featured edge lettering as a distinctive element. Missing edge lettering errors are particularly notable because they represent a failure in one of the final stages of the minting process.

Rarity and Market Value:

Coins with missing edge lettering, especially from the earlier years of the Presidential Dollar series, are highly sought after. They can range widely in value, typically selling for $50 to $100, with exceptional examples or those in uncirculated condition fetching higher prices.

2009
Zachary Taylor Dollar
"Lettering Error"

Detailed Description:

This specific error includes misspelled or misplaced inscriptions along the edge of the coin. Some examples include double lettering or inverted inscriptions, which make these coins unique among collectibles.

Historical Context:

The Zachary Taylor Dollar was part of the ongoing Presidential Dollar series, which experienced several minting quirks due to the complexity of applying edge lettering post-strike. Errors from this specific production year highlight the ongoing challenges faced by the U.S. Mint in consistently applying new technologies.

Rarity and Market Value:

Edge lettering errors, particularly those involving misprints or double strikes, are quite rare and can be valuable, typically fetching $100 to $300, with particularly unique or striking errors commanding even higher prices.

Colonial Coin Errors

1787
Fugio Cent "Cinquefoil" Error

Detailed Description:

The Fugio Cent, one of the earliest coins issued by the United States, occasionally featured errors such as the "Cinquefoil" error. This error is characterized by extra or malformed decorative elements around the sundial. The term "Cinquefoil" refers to a design intended to resemble five leaves or petals, but errors in the minting process led to variations where these elements are improperly formed or duplicated.

Historical Context:

Minted in 1787, the Fugio Cent was designed by Benjamin Franklin and reflects the nascent identity of the United States. The coin's design includes the sun and sundial with the motto "Fugio" ("I fly") and "Mind Your Business," signifying the passage of time and the importance of industriousness. Errors like the "Cinquefoil" are a testament to the primitive minting techniques and quality control challenges of the era.

Rarity and Market Value:

Errors on colonial coins like the Fugio Cent are extremely rare and highly sought after. The value of a 1787 Fugio Cent with the "Cinquefoil" error can vary greatly, often exceeding several thousand dollars, depending on the coin's condition and the clarity of the error. Well-preserved examples with prominent errors are particularly valuable.

1723
Hibernia Halfpenny "Double Struck" Error

Detailed Description:

The 1723 Hibernia Halfpenny, minted for circulation in the American colonies, sometimes displays a "Double Struck" error. This occurs when the coin is struck twice by the die, resulting in a slight overlapping of the design elements. This double impression is especially noticeable around the edges of the coin, where the letters and figures appear blurred or shadowed.

Historical Context:

Hibernia Halfpennies were produced under contract in England and shipped to the American colonies to alleviate the chronic shortage of small denomination coins. Errors like double striking were relatively common due to the manual and imprecise nature of the minting process.

Rarity and Market Value:

Double struck Hibernia Halfpennies are prized by collectors for their historical significance and visual appeal. Depending on the clarity of the double strike and the coin's overall condition, these errors can fetch prices ranging from $200 to over $1,000.

1652
Massachusetts Pine Tree Shilling "Off-Center" Error

Detailed Description:

The Massachusetts Pine Tree Shilling, minted in the mid-17th century, occasionally exhibits "Off-Center" errors. These errors occur when the coin blank is not properly aligned with the die during striking, resulting in a design that is shifted to one side, leaving part of the coin blank or with incomplete imagery.

Historical Context:

The Pine Tree Shilling is one of the most iconic early American coins, minted by the Massachusetts Bay Colony without official sanction from the English crown. The off-center errors provide a glimpse into the early colonial minting practices, which were often rudimentary and prone to inconsistencies.

Rarity and Market Value:

Off-center Pine Tree Shillings are exceptionally rare and highly coveted. The value of such coins can be substantial, often ranging from $2,000 to $10,000 or more, depending on the degree of the error and the coin's condition.

1788
Vermont Copper "Double Struck" Error

Detailed Description:

The 1788 Vermont Copper coin, part of the early state coinage, sometimes features a "Double Struck" error. Similar to the Hibernia Halfpenny, this error occurs when the coin is struck twice, resulting in overlapping design elements. The doubling is typically evident in the lettering and the central motifs of the coin.

Historical Context:

Vermont Copper coins were minted by private contractors before Vermont became a state. The coins were widely used in local commerce and reflect the economic conditions and minting capabilities of the period. Errors like double striking highlight the challenges faced by early American minters.

Rarity and Market Value:

Double struck Vermont Coppers are sought after by collectors for their uniqueness and historical value. These coins can range in value from $500 to several thousand dollars, depending on the sharpness of the doubling and the overall state of preservation.

Small Gold Coin Errors

1849
Liberty Head Gold Dollar "Clipped Planchet" Error

Detailed Description:

The 1849 Liberty Head Gold Dollar sometimes features a "Clipped Planchet" error, where a portion of the coin's edge is missing due to the planchet (the blank metal disk used for striking the coin) being improperly cut. This results in a noticeable crescent-shaped missing piece along the coin's edge.

Historical Context:

The Liberty Head Gold Dollar was introduced in 1849 as part of the first gold dollar series minted by the United States. During this period, the minting process was still evolving, and errors like clipped planchets were relatively common. These errors occurred when the cutting machines misaligned, causing the blanks to overlap during the cutting process.

Rarity and Market Value:

Clipped planchet errors are rare and desirable among collectors, especially on gold coins due to their intrinsic value. The value of an 1849 Liberty Head Gold Dollar with a clipped planchet can range from $500 to $5,000, depending on the size of the clip and the coin's overall condition.

1854
Indian Princess Gold Dollar "Double Die Obverse" Error

Detailed Description:

This error is characterized by noticeable doubling on the obverse side of the coin, affecting the features of the Indian Princess and the inscriptions. The doubling gives the design elements a shadowed or blurred appearance, making the error easily recognizable.

Historical Context:

The Indian Princess Gold Dollar series, introduced in 1854, replaced the Liberty Head design. The double die obverse error occurred during the die hubbing process, where the die received multiple, slightly misaligned impressions. This type of error was not uncommon during the 19th century, when quality control measures were less stringent than today.

Rarity and Market Value:

Double die obverse errors on gold dollars are highly prized due to their visual appeal and rarity. An 1854 Indian Princess Gold Dollar with a double die obverse can command prices ranging from $1,000 to over $10,000, depending on the clarity of the doubling and the coin's grade.

1908
Indian Head Quarter Eagle
"Weak D" Mintmark Error

No image available

Detailed Description:

The 1908 Indian Head Quarter Eagle often exhibits a "Weak D" mintmark error, where the "D" mintmark (denoting the Denver Mint) is faint or partially struck. This error results from insufficient pressure during the striking process or debris obstructing the die.

Historical Context:

The Indian Head Quarter Eagle series began in 1908, featuring an incuse (recessed) design, which was unique at the time. The weak D mintmark error provides insight into the challenges faced during the early production of this innovative design.

Rarity and Market Value:

Coins with a weak D mintmark are sought after by collectors, particularly those focusing on mintmark varieties. The value of a 1908 Indian Head Quarter Eagle with a weak D mintmark typically ranges from $300 to $3,000, depending on the visibility of the mintmark and the coin's condition.

1911-D
Indian Head Quarter Eagle
"Overdate" Error

No image available

Detailed Description:

The 1911-D Indian Head Quarter Eagle features an "Overdate" error, where the date appears to have been stamped over a previous date, resulting in a doubled or blurred appearance. This error is a result of a die being repurposed with a new date without completely removing the old one.

Historical Context:

The overdate errors were relatively common in the early 20th century as the U.S. Mint occasionally reused dies to save on production costs. The 1911-D overdate is one of the more notable examples from this period.

Rarity and Market Value:

Overdate errors are particularly valued by numismatists due to their historical significance and rarity. A 1911-D Indian Head Quarter Eagle with an overdate error can fetch between $1,500 and $15,000, depending on the extent of the overdate and the coin's grade.

Large Gold Coin Errors

1849
Liberty Head Double Eagle
"Broadstrike" Error

Detailed Description:

The 1849 Liberty Head Double Eagle can sometimes be found with a "Broadstrike" error, where the coin was struck without the retaining collar that gives the coin its proper shape and diameter. This results in a coin that is larger in diameter with a flattened, expanded design, often lacking the usual raised rim.

Historical Context:

The Liberty Head Double Eagle, introduced in 1849, was part of the United States' response to the California Gold Rush, which significantly increased the nation's gold supply. The broadstrike error illustrates the minting challenges during this period of rapid expansion and increased demand for coinage.

Rarity and Market Value:

Broadstrike errors on large gold coins like the Double Eagle are quite rare due to the robust quality control measures typically employed during the minting process. The value of an 1849 Liberty Head Double Eagle with a broadstrike error can range from $5,000 to $20,000 or more, depending on the coin's condition and the prominence of the error.

1876
Liberty Head Double Eagle
"Double Die Obverse" Error

Detailed Description:

This error is characterized by noticeable doubling on the obverse side of the coin, particularly affecting Liberty's profile and the surrounding stars and inscriptions. The double die error gives these elements a blurred or shadowed appearance, making the error highly visible.

Historical Context:

The Liberty Head Double Eagle, minted from 1849 to 1907, was a crucial part of U.S. gold coinage. The double die obverse error occurred due to multiple, slightly misaligned impressions during the die-making process, a common issue before the advent of modern minting technologies.

Rarity and Market Value:

Double die obverse errors on Liberty Head Double Eagles are highly prized by collectors for their rarity and historical significance. The value of an 1876 Double Eagle with a double die obverse can range from $10,000 to over $50,000, depending on the coin's condition and the clarity of the doubling.

1907
Saint-Gaudens Double Eagle "High Relief" Error

Detailed Description:

The 1907 Saint-Gaudens Double Eagle was initially struck in high relief, which required multiple strikes to fully bring up the design. Some of these coins exhibit errors where the relief is either unusually high or uneven, resulting in a strikingly three-dimensional appearance that is not uniform across the coin.

Historical Context:

Designed by Augustus Saint-Gaudens, the 1907 Double Eagle is considered one of the most beautiful coins ever minted by the United States. The high relief design proved challenging for the minting process, leading to significant modifications in later issues to facilitate mass production.

Rarity and Market Value:

High relief errors are particularly significant due to their association with the transition from the initial high relief to the more practical low relief design. Coins with these errors can command prices ranging from $20,000 to several hundred thousand dollars, depending on their condition and the extent of the error.

1920
Saint-Gaudens Double Eagle "Weak Strike" Error

Detailed Description:

This error is characterized by a noticeably weak strike, where the details of the design are not fully brought up, giving the coin a softer, less defined appearance. This can be seen in the features of Liberty, the rays of the sun, and the eagle on the reverse.

Historical Context:

The Saint-Gaudens Double Eagle series, minted from 1907 to 1933, faced various production challenges. The weak strike error highlights the occasional issues with the striking pressure or die condition, especially during periods of high demand or equipment wear.

Rarity and Market Value:

Weak strike errors on Saint-Gaudens Double Eagles are relatively uncommon and are valued for their unique appearance and insight into the minting process. These coins can range in value from $5,000 to $50,000, depending on the severity of the weak strike and the overall condition of the coin.

Bullion Gold Eagle Errors

1795
Capped Bust Right Eagle "Reversed Eagle" Error

Detailed Description:

The 1795 Capped Bust Right Eagle features an early minting error known as the "Reversed Eagle" error, where the eagle on the reverse side is incorrectly oriented. This error occurs due to a misalignment of the dies during the striking process, resulting in the eagle facing the wrong direction.

Historical Context:

The 1795 Capped Bust Right Eagle was among the first gold eagles minted by the United States. This era was marked by the infancy of the U.S. Mint and its evolving minting technology. Errors like the "Reversed Eagle" highlight the challenges faced in standardizing coin production.

Rarity and Market Value:

Reversed Eagle errors are extremely rare and hold significant value due to their historical importance. The market value for such coins can range from $50,000 to over $250,000, heavily dependent on the coin's condition and the prominence of the error.

1801
Capped Bust Right Eagle "Broadstrike" Error

Detailed Description:

The 1801 Capped Bust Right Eagle occasionally displays a "Broadstrike" error, where the coin is struck outside the collar, resulting in a larger-than-normal diameter and a distorted or flattened appearance. This error occurs when the retaining collar fails to properly align the planchet during striking.

Historical Context:

The early 1800s were a period of refining minting techniques. The broadstrike error is indicative of the manual processes involved and the technical difficulties encountered. Such errors provide a glimpse into the mint's operational struggles during this formative period.

Rarity and Market Value:

Broadstrike errors on early gold eagles are particularly rare. Coins with this error can command prices ranging from $20,000 to $100,000 or more, depending on their condition and the extent of the error.

1839
Liberty Head Eagle "Misplaced Date" Error

No image available

Detailed Description:

The 1839 Liberty Head Eagle sometimes features a "Misplaced Date" error, where the date appears out of alignment or partially struck in an incorrect area of the coin. This error results from improper positioning of the date punch during the die preparation.

Historical Context:

The Liberty Head Eagle series began in 1838, marking a new design era for U.S. gold coinage. Misplaced date errors from this period reflect the transitional nature of minting practices and the human error involved in manual die engraving.

Rarity and Market Value:

Misplaced date errors on Liberty Head Eagles are highly collectible and can vary significantly in value. Prices typically range from $10,000 to $50,000, depending on the visibility of the error and the coin's overall condition.

1907
Indian Head Eagle "Wire Rim" Error

Detailed Description:

The 1907 Indian Head Eagle, designed by Augustus Saint-Gaudens, is known for its "Wire Rim" error, where a thin, raised line of metal appears around the edge of the coin. This error occurred during the initial high-relief strikes, where the excessive metal flow created the wire rim.

Historical Context:

The Indian Head Eagle was part of a broader initiative to beautify American coinage. The 1907 issues were struck in high relief, which proved problematic for mass production. The wire rim is a result of the mint's experimentation with the new design.

Rarity and Market Value:

Wire rim errors are highly sought after due to their association with Saint-Gaudens' original design and the challenges of high-relief minting. These coins can fetch prices from $15,000 to over $100,000, with the value depending on the error's prominence and the coin's grade.

1920-S
Saint-Gaudens Double Eagle "Weak Strike" Error

Detailed Description:

This error is characterized by a weak strike, where the design details, particularly on Liberty and the eagle, are not fully formed. This occurs due to insufficient striking pressure or worn dies, leading to a less defined and softer appearance.

Historical Context:

The 1920s were a turbulent time for the U.S. economy and the minting operations, with fluctuating gold demands and changing technologies. Weak strikes from this period reflect the operational pressures and resource constraints faced by the mint.

Rarity and Market Value:

Weak strike errors on Saint-Gaudens Double Eagles are relatively uncommon and are valued for their uniqueness. Prices for such coins can range from $5,000 to $50,000, depending on the extent of the weak strike and the coin's overall condition.

Additional Considerations for Collecting

Documentation and Certification: For collectors of error coins, especially in the categories of colonial, gold, and bullion, obtaining well-documented and certified examples is crucial due to the rarity and value of these coins. Certification by reputable services like PCGS or NGC can authenticate the error and help in accurately assessing the coin's market value.

Market Fluctuations: The value of gold and bullion coins can be significantly affected by precious metal prices, while the rarity and historical value primarily drive the value of colonial coins. Collectors must consider both aspects when acquiring, selling, or valuing their collections.

Historical Research: For colonial and historical gold coins, further research into the provenance and historical context of each piece can add to both the enjoyment of collecting and the potential investment value. Books, auction catalogs, and academic papers can provide invaluable information.

This chapter has explored some of the most fascinating and valuable error coins, providing collectors with detailed insights into the quirks of the minting process and the potential value of these anomalies. Collecting error coins is not only a hobby but also a form of historical preservation, capturing unique moments in minting history that are as instructive as they are valuable.

3

Hidden Histories

The world of numismatics is filled with fascinating tales of rare and valuable coins, but perhaps none are quite as intriguing as the stories behind error coins. These numismatic oddities, born from mistakes in the minting process, offer a unique window into the complexities of coin production and the quirks of history. In this chapter, we'll delve into the captivating stories behind specific error coins, explore the historical events and circumstances that led to their creation, and share personal anecdotes from mint workers and lucky discoverers.

Detailed stories behind specific error coins

1. The 1955 Double Die Obverse Lincoln Cent

One of the most famous and sought-after error coins in American numismatics is the 1955 Double Die Obverse Lincoln Cent. This penny features a dramatic doubling of the date, motto, and lettering on the obverse (heads) side of the coin, creating a striking and unmistakable error.

The story of this coin begins late one night at the Philadelphia Mint in 1955. The mint was working overtime to meet the high demand for pennies, and in the rush to produce more dies, a crucial mistake was made. When creating the hub (the master die used to make working dies), the design was impressed twice at slightly different angles, creating a doubled image on the working dies.

By the time the error was discovered, around 20,000 to 24,000 of these double die cents had already been minted and mixed with normal pennies. Rather than destroy the coins and waste the resources, mint officials made the unusual decision to release them into circulation. They reasoned that the coins would be gradually discovered and removed from circulation by collectors, minimizing any public confusion.

The decision proved fateful for numismatics. Today, the 1955 Double Die Obverse cent is one of the most valuable Lincoln cents, with well-preserved specimens fetching tens of thousands of dollars at auction. Its dramatic appearance and scarcity have made it a holy grail for many coin collectors.

2. The 1943 Copper Penny

In the midst of World War II, the United States Mint faced a critical shortage of copper, which was needed for the war effort. To conserve this vital metal, the mint switched to producing pennies made of zinc-coated steel for the year 1943. However, a tiny number of copper planchets (coin blanks) left over from 1942 somehow made their way into the presses, resulting in a few 1943 pennies struck in copper instead of steel.

For years, the existence of these copper 1943 pennies was the subject of rumor and speculation. The story gained traction when Henry Ford supposedly offered a free car to anyone who could produce one, although this was likely an urban legend. Nevertheless, the hunt was on, and over time, a small number of genuine 1943 copper cents were discovered.

The rarity of these coins cannot be overstated. It's estimated that no more than 40 copper cents were struck in 1943 across all three mints (Philadelphia, Denver, and San Francisco). Of these, only about 20 are known to exist today. The value of these coins is astronomical, with one specimen selling for over $1 million in 2010.

The story of the 1943 copper penny illustrates how even small oversights in the minting process, especially during times of great change or stress, can result in numismatic treasures. It also serves as a reminder of the sacrifices and material shortages faced by Americans during World War II.

3. The 2004 Wisconsin State Quarter with Extra Leaf

The 50 State Quarters Program, which ran from 1999 to 2008, was one of the most popular coin initiatives in U.S. history. However, it also produced one of the most intriguing modern coin errors: the 2004 Wisconsin quarter with an extra leaf on the ear of corn.

The Wisconsin quarter design features a cow, a wheel of cheese, and an ear of corn, emblems of the state's agricultural heritage. In late 2004, collectors began to notice something odd about some Wisconsin quarters: an additional leaf appeared to be sprouting from the corn husks. Two varieties were identified: the "Low Leaf" and the "High Leaf."

Initial speculation ran wild. Some thought it might be an intentional "Easter egg" hidden by the designer, while others suspected sabotage by a rogue mint employee. The truth, as often happens, was more mundane but no less interesting.

Investigation by the U.S. Mint determined that the extra leaf was likely caused by damage to the die. Theory suggests that a small piece of metal, perhaps from a broken piece of equipment, became lodged in the die, creating the illusion of an extra leaf. As the die wore down during the minting process, the shape of this foreign object changed slightly, accounting for the two different "leaf" positions.

It's estimated that between 50,000 to 100,000 of these error coins entered circulation before the problem was caught. While not as rare as some other errors, the Wisconsin extra leaf quarters remain popular with collectors due to their distinctive appearance and the mystery surrounding their creation.

4. The 2007 Presidential Dollar with Missing Edge Lettering

When the Presidential $1 Coin Program launched in 2007, it introduced a new minting process for U.S. coins. Unlike previous dollars, the edge lettering (which includes the motto "In God We Trust," "E Pluribus Unum," and the year of minting) was to be applied in a separate step after the main striking of the coin.

This new process led to a notable error in the first year of production. Some coins, now known as "Godless Dollars," were released without the edge lettering. The missing "In God We Trust" motto caused a minor controversy and garnered significant media attention.

The error occurred because some planchets somehow bypassed the edge-lettering machine or went through without being struck. Estimates suggest that about 50,000 George Washington dollars were released without edge lettering.

This error highlighted the challenges of introducing new minting technologies and processes. It also demonstrated how even in the modern era of highly automated coin production, errors can and do occur. The incident led to increased quality control measures at the mint and a redesign of the coins in subsequent years, with "In God We Trust" moved to the obverse to prevent similar errors.

5. The 1937-D Three-Legged Buffalo Nickel

The Buffalo nickel, minted from 1913 to 1938, is one of the most iconic American coin designs. However, a minting error in 1937 at the Denver Mint created one of the most famous and sought-after varieties of this coin: the Three-Legged Buffalo.

On normal Buffalo nickels, the bison on the reverse has four legs. But on this error variety, the buffalo appears to be standing on only three legs, with the front right leg mostly missing.

The error occurred due to overzealous die polishing. During the minting process, dies would occasionally develop defects or buildup that needed to be polished away. In this case, a mint employee accidentally polished too aggressively, essentially erasing most of the buffalo's front right leg from the die.

What makes this error particularly interesting is that it went unnoticed for some time, allowing a significant number of these "three-legged" nickels to enter circulation. Estimates suggest that about 100,000 were minted before the error was caught and the die replaced.

The Three-Legged Buffalo has since become one of the most famous and valuable error coins in American numismatics. Its distinctive appearance, coupled with its relative scarcity, has made it a prized possession for collectors of Buffalo nickels and error coins alike.

These stories represent just a small sampling of the fascinating world of error coins. Each mistake, each oversight, each quirk of fate that leads to the creation of these numismatic oddities adds a chapter to the rich tapestry of minting history. They remind us that even in processes designed to produce millions of identical items, the unexpected can and does happen, often with remarkable results.

Historical events and minting circumstances leading to errors

Error coins are not created in a vacuum. Often, they are the result of unique historical circumstances, technological changes, or even societal pressures. Understanding the context in which these errors occurred can provide valuable insights into both numismatic history and broader historical events.

1. Wartime Production and Material Shortages

World War II had a profound impact on coin production in many countries, leading to a variety of interesting errors and varieties. We've already discussed the 1943 copper cent, but this was just one example of how wartime demands affected coinage.

In the United States, the war effort required vast amounts of copper and nickel, both key components in coin production. This led to the creation of the steel cent in 1943 and the silver "war nickel" from 1942 to 1945. The rapid changes in materials and production methods increased the likelihood of errors.

Similar situations occurred in other countries. In the UK, the composition of the penny was changed from bronze to steel in 1941 to save copper for the war effort. This change led to a number of minting difficulties and resultant errors, including weakly struck coins and issues with rusting.

In Germany, as the war progressed and resources became scarcer, the quality of coin production declined significantly. This led to an increase in weakly struck coins, off-center strikes, and other errors. Some of the most interesting error coins from this period are the so-called "defeat marks," where Allied troops deliberately damaged dies to create subtle errors in Nazi coinage as an act of resistance.

2. The Transition to Clad Coinage

In the mid-1960s, rising silver prices forced many countries, including the United States, to abandon silver for everyday coinage. The U.S. Mint transitioned to clad coinage - coins with a copper core sandwiched between layers of nickel - for dimes and quarters in 1965, and for half dollars in 1971.

This major change in production methods led to a variety of transitional errors. Some of the most valuable are the "transitional errors" where a coin was struck on the wrong planchet type. For example, some 1964-dated coins were struck on the new clad planchets, while some 1965-dated coins were struck on silver planchets left over from the previous year.

The introduction of clad coinage also led to a new type of error: the "clad separation" error. In these cases, the outer layer of the coin separates from the inner core, creating a distinctive and visually striking error.

3. The Great Depression and the Hoover Dam Medal

The Great Depression had far-reaching effects on every aspect of American life, including coin production. Mint output decreased dramatically as the demand for currency dropped. However, this period also saw the creation of one of the most infamous error medals in U.S. history.

In 1935, to commemorate the completion of the Hoover Dam, the Denver Mint struck a series of medals. Due to a spelling error, the first batch of these medals misspelled "Beverly Hills" as "Beverley Hills" on the reverse. The error was quickly caught and corrected, but not before a number of these misspelled medals had been distributed.

This error, while seemingly minor, encapsulates the challenges faced by the Mint during this difficult period. With resources stretched thin and morale low, even simple proofreading errors could slip through the cracks.

4. The Decimalisation of British Currency

In 1971, the United Kingdom underwent a major currency reform, switching from the centuries-old system of pounds, shillings, and pence to a decimal system. This massive undertaking required the production of millions of new coins and the withdrawal of the old coinage from circulation.

The pressure to produce such a large quantity of new coins in a relatively short time led to an increase in minting errors. One of the most notable was the 1983 "New Pence" two pence coin. After decimalisation, two pence coins were supposed to read "Two Pence," but in 1983, a batch was mistakenly struck using an old die that still read "New Pence." These error coins are now highly sought after by collectors.

5. The Introduction of the Euro

The introduction of the Euro in 2002 was one of the largest currency changeovers in history, affecting multiple countries simultaneously. The massive scale of this operation, combined with the need for secrecy in the lead-up to the launch, created conditions ripe for minting errors.

One of the most famous Euro errors occurred in the Netherlands. A small number of 2002 Dutch 1 euro coins were struck with the internal part of the bi-metallic coin rotated 180 degrees relative to the outer part. These "rotated die" errors are now highly prized by Euro coin collectors.

6. The 50 State Quarters Program

The 50 State Quarters Program, which ran from 1999 to 2008, was the most extensive coin redesign in U.S. history. With a new reverse design being introduced every 10 weeks for a decade, the potential for errors was significantly increased.

We've already discussed the Wisconsin quarter with the extra leaf, but there were other interesting errors as well. For example, some 2005 Kansas quarters were struck with a distinctive die crack that made it appear as if the bison on the reverse had a "hump back."

The State Quarters Program also saw an increase in "mule" errors - coins struck with mismatched dies. The most famous of these is the 2000 "Sacagawea Mule," where a small number of Sacagawea dollar planchets were struck with a State quarter obverse die.

7. The Rise of Automation

The increasing automation of the minting process throughout the 20th and 21st centuries has generally led to greater consistency and fewer errors. However, when errors do occur in an automated system, they can sometimes be produced in large numbers before being detected.

A prime example is the 2004-2005 Westward Journey nickel series, which saw a higher-than-usual number of errors due to the frequent design changes and the challenges of striking the new designs. Some of these errors, like weakly struck coins or misaligned dies, were produced in significant quantities before being caught.

8. Environmental Factors

Sometimes, minting errors can be caused by factors entirely outside of the minting process itself. In 1922, a severe snowstorm in Denver led to an interesting variety of Lincoln cents. The storm forced the mint to close briefly, and when it reopened, many of the dies were found to be rusted. Rather than discard them, mint officials decided to polish the dies to remove the rust. This polishing was sometimes overzealous, leading to coins where the mint mark was either very faint or completely absent. These "1922 No D" cents are now highly prized by collectors.

Understanding these historical contexts adds depth to our appreciation of error coins. They are not just numismatic curiosities, but tangible links to specific moments in history, reflecting the

challenges, changes, and sometimes chaotic circumstances of their times. Whether it's wartime material shortages, massive currency reforms, or simply the everyday challenges of producing millions of coins, each error tells a story that goes beyond the coin itself.

Personal anecdotes from mint workers and discoverers

The human element in the creation and discovery of error coins adds a fascinating dimension to their stories. While mint workers are generally tight-lipped about the details of their work, and many discoveries happen anonymously, there are still some compelling personal accounts that have made their way into numismatic lore.

1. The Mint Worker's Dilemma

In the late 1980s, a worker at the Philadelphia Mint, whose name has been withheld for privacy, shared an interesting anecdote about error detection. He described the conflicting emotions felt by many mint workers when they spot an error:

"You're trained to catch mistakes, and you take pride in producing perfect coins. But there's always this tiny voice in the back of your head when you see an error. Part of you wants to let it slip through, knowing it could become something special. But professional integrity always wins out. Still, I often wonder about the errors I caught that could have been the next big thing in collecting."

This account highlights the human aspect of quality control in minting and the tension between professional responsibility and the allure of numismatic fame.

2. The Accidental Discovery of the 1969-S Doubled Die Obverse Lincoln Cent

One of the most valuable modern error coins, the 1969-S Doubled Die Obverse Lincoln Cent, was discovered quite by accident. In 1970, a coin collector named John Wexler was going through rolls of pennies looking for a 1960 Small Date cent to complete his collection. Instead, he found something unexpected.

Wexler recounts: "I couldn't believe my eyes. At first, I thought it was a fake because the doubling was so pronounced. But after careful examination, I realized I had stumbled upon something truly special. It just goes to show, you never know what you might find in a simple roll of pennies from the bank."

Wexler's discovery kicked off a frenzy among collectors, and to this day, the 1969-S Doubled Die Obverse cent remains one of the most sought-after Lincoln cent varieties.

3. The Denver Mint Mishap

An anonymous former employee of the Denver Mint shared a story about an incident in the 1990s that nearly led to a major error release:

"We had just started a new run of quarters when someone noticed something off about the rings around the edge. Turns out, the machine that adds the reeding (the ridges on the edge of the coin) was misaligned. We caught it quickly, but for about 15 minutes, we were minting quarters with partial reeding. It was a tense few hours as we had to account for every single one of those coins. As far as I know, we got them all, but sometimes I wonder if a few might have slipped through."

This anecdote gives us a glimpse into the high-pressure environment of a working mint and the constant vigilance required to prevent errors from entering circulation.

4. The Lucky Cashier

Not all discoveries are made by serious collectors. Sometimes, ordinary people stumble upon extraordinary finds. Sarah Johnson, a cashier at a small convenience store in Ohio, shares her unexpected encounter with a valuable error coin:

"It was just another day at work in 2005 when I noticed something odd about a quarter in my till. The Wisconsin state quarter had what looked like an extra leaf on the corn. I remembered reading something about this in the newspaper, so I decided to keep it and swap it out with one of my own quarters. That coin ended up paying for a good chunk of my college tuition!"

Sarah's story is a reminder that error coins can be found anywhere, and a little knowledge can lead to a life-changing discovery.

5. The Mint Director's Nightmare

A former director of the U.S. Mint, speaking on condition of anonymity, shared the stress of dealing with major error releases:

"The 2004 Wisconsin quarter error was a real wake-up call for us. When reports started coming in about the extra leaf varieties, we had to act fast. We launched an internal investigation, reviewed our quality control procedures, and had to prepare statements for the press. It's a delicate balance – we need to maintain public trust in our currency while also acknowledging that, despite our best efforts, errors can happen. Those were some sleepless nights, let me tell you."

This perspective from a high-level mint official underscores the serious implications that major error releases can have, going far beyond the excitement they generate in the collecting community.

6. The Collector's Persistence

Sometimes, the story behind the discovery of an error coin is as much about persistence as it is about luck. Tom Wolfe, a dedicated coin collector from California, shares his experience of finding a valuable error after years of searching:

"I had been collecting State quarters since the program began in 1999. In 2005, I heard about the Kansas quarter with the 'In God We Rust' error – where part of the 'T' in 'TRUST' was filled in. I made it my mission to find one. For months, I went through every quarter that passed through my hands. I even convinced my local bank to let me search through their quarter rolls. After almost a year of searching, I finally found one. The feeling was indescribable – a mix of excitement, relief, and vindication. It taught me that in coin collecting, patience and persistence really do pay off."

Tom's story illustrates the dedication of many collectors and the thrill of finally finding that elusive error after a long search.

7. The Mint Employee's Close Call

A retired Philadelphia Mint employee shared a story about a near-miss that could have resulted in a major error coin release:

"It was in the late 1990s, and we were producing dimes. Someone had accidentally mixed a batch of penny planchets in with the dime planchets. We caught it pretty quickly, but not before a few hundred copper-colored dimes were struck. There was a mad scramble to find and destroy them all. As far as I know, we got them all, but there's always that nagging thought – what if one got out? It would be an incredible find for some lucky collector."

This story highlights how even small mistakes in the minting process can potentially create highly valuable numismatic rarities.

These personal anecdotes add a human dimension to the world of error coins. They remind us that behind every minting error, there's a story of oversight, discovery, or near-miss. From the mint workers striving for perfection to the collectors and everyday people who stumble upon these numismatic treasures, these stories enrich our understanding and appreciation of error coins.

Error coins are more than just mistakes – they're unintended windows into the minting process, capsules of historical circumstances, and objects of fascination for collectors and historians alike. As we've explored in this chapter, the stories behind these coins are often as valuable and interesting as the coins themselves, adding depth and context to the world of numismatics.

4

Expert Insights

Interviews with Numismatists, Mint Employees, and Collectors

Exploring the nuanced world of error coins through the eyes of those deeply embedded in its culture—numismatists, mint employees, and seasoned collectors—offers a unique perspective that enriches our understanding. These individuals provide a wealth of knowledge and firsthand insights that illuminate both the technical and personal aspects of collecting error coins.

Insights from a Leading Numismatist

Dr. Helena Markson, a numismatist with over thirty years of experience, specializes in error coins. She shares her deep appreciation for these unique collectibles: "Each error coin holds a story, frozen in metal, a testament to the fleeting imperfection in the minting process." Dr. Markson has contributed to numerous scholarly articles and authored several pivotal books that discuss the intricacies of error coins. According to her, the key to appreciating error coins lies in understanding how they are made and recognizing the rarity and uniqueness of each error. "Studying these coins opens a window into the often-hidden aspects of the minting world and shows us that beauty can indeed be found in mistakes."

Dr. Markson elaborates on the importance of technical knowledge in appreciating error coins, explaining that "understanding the specific mechanical or human error that led to the coin's uniqueness can significantly enhance its value to a collector." She emphasizes that the errors are not just flaws but also opportunities for learning and appreciation of the minting process's complexity.

Experience from a Mint Production Manager

John Cartwright has been at the forefront of coin production at the U.S. Mint for over two decades. His role involves overseeing the journey of a coin from design to distribution, ensuring each step meets the stringent standards set by the Mint. "Errors are rare, but they're fascinating because they highlight the human element in our work," Cartwright explains. He recalls a particular incident where a slight delay in the die setup led to several hundred misstruck coins. "Such moments remind us that the process is as much an art as it is a science. Each error, while a mistake, adds a unique chapter to the history of minting."

Cartwright discusses the challenges and pressures of maintaining the mint's high standards. "Every day, we strive to strike millions of coins, each one meant to be a perfect ambassador of the U.S. Mint. When an error slips through, it's a humbling reminder of our mission and the precision required." His stories shed light on the delicate balance of maintaining traditional craftsmanship in an increasingly automated industry.

Stories from a Dedicated Collector

Maria Gonzalez, who started collecting coins as a hobby and now curates one of the most enviable collections of error coins, recounts her first encounter with a double-denominated coin—a nickel struck on a penny planchet. "It was purely accidental, found in a roll of coins from a local bank. That moment changed the course of my collecting journey," she shares. Maria emphasizes the thrill of the hunt and the community aspect of collecting, "Connecting with other collectors, sharing finds and stories—it's a community that values history and the thrill of discovery."

Gonzalez also reflects on how each error coin in her collection represents a specific moment in minting history. "Every coin tells a story, not just about the error, but about the time it was made, the people who made it, and how it came to be discovered," she says. Her passion for the stories behind the coins is palpable and is a significant part of what drives her continuous pursuit of new and unusual pieces.

These interviews underscore the multifaceted allure of error coins, blending technical mastery, historical significance, and personal passion. Through their experiences and stories, these experts and enthusiasts provide a comprehensive view of the world of error coins, from the technicalities of their creation to the personal joys and challenges of collecting them. This blend of perspectives not only deepens our appreciation for error coins but also highlights the rich tapestry of human endeavor that they represent within the broader narrative of numismatics.

Tips and Advice from Experts on Identifying and Valuing Error Coins

Identifying and valuing error coins is an art form that requires knowledge, patience, and a keen eye for detail. Experts from various corners of the numismatic world offer advice that can help both novice and seasoned collectors refine their skills in spotting and appreciating these unique coins.

Understanding Error Coin Categories

Dr. Helena Markson, a veteran numismatist, emphasizes the importance of understanding the various categories of error coins. "Knowledge of different error types—planchet, die, striking, and others—is crucial. It helps in identifying what makes each coin special and can significantly affect its value." She suggests that collectors familiarize themselves with the definitions and characteristics of common errors such as double strikes, off-centers, and die varieties to better understand what to look for.

"Understanding the nuances between a double die and a double strike, for example, can significantly impact both the appraisal and the historical importance of a coin," Dr. Markson explains. Double dies occur during the die-making process, while double strikes happen during the coin striking process, each bringing its unique form of rarity and collector interest.

Tools for the Trade

For error coin collectors, having the right tools can make a significant difference. "Invest in a good magnifying glass or a digital microscope," advises John Cartwright, a seasoned mint production manager. These tools allow collectors to examine potential error coins in detail, which is essential for accurate identification and valuation. A precision scale and caliper can also be invaluable for detecting subtle differences in weight and size that might indicate an error.

"Sometimes, the errors are microscopic, and without proper magnification, they can easily be missed," says Cartwright. He also suggests investing in proper lighting, as some features can only be seen under direct light, or at certain angles, highlighting the importance of a well-equipped workspace for examination.

Authenticating and Grading Error Coins

Given the value and rarity of many error coins, ensuring their authenticity and condition is paramount. "Always opt for reputable third-party grading services," recommends Maria Gonzalez, a prominent collector known for her extensive error coin collection. These services not only verify the authenticity of coins but also grade them, which helps in establishing their market value. "A graded error coin often carries more credibility and is easier to sell or trade," she adds.

Gonzalez shares that third-party grading not only helps in confirming the authenticity but also in protecting the coin. "Once encased by a professional grading service, the coin is preserved from further wear, which is crucial for maintaining its value over time," she notes.

Learning from Mistakes

Mistakes are part of the learning process, even in collecting. "I once overpaid for what I thought was a rare error coin that turned out to be a manipulated regular coin," shares Dr. Markson. Such experiences are teaching moments. "Every mistake provides valuable lessons. More importantly, they teach you to be more diligent and thorough in your research and verification," she notes.

She advises collectors to always ask for documentation and provenance when possible, and to build a network of trusted experts whom they can turn to for advice or second opinions. "Collecting is not just about acquiring; it's about understanding and learning. Each piece in your collection should tell a story, one that you're ready to share accurately and proudly," Dr. Markson adds.

Pricing and Market Dynamics

The market for error coins can be volatile, with prices heavily influenced by rarity, demand, and the coin's error type. "Stay informed about market trends," advises Cartwright. "Auctions, trade shows, and numismatic publications are good resources for keeping up with how error coins are valued in the market." He also suggests that collectors develop relationships with knowledgeable dealers and fellow collectors who can offer insights and advice.

Cartwright notes that part of understanding market dynamics involves recognizing that the error coin market is niche. "Not every collector goes for error coins. They appeal to those who appreciate the oddities and the stories behind the minting mistakes. Therefore, the community, while smaller, is often very passionate and knowledgeable."

These expert tips form a foundation for both understanding and navigating the complex world of error coins. With the right knowledge and tools, collectors can enhance their ability to not only identify and value these unique pieces but also to appreciate the broader narrative they represent in the numismatic community.

Through detailed interviews with hands-on advice, this chapter equips readers with a comprehensive understanding of error coins, fostering a deeper appreciation for this intriguing aspect of numismatics. Through expert insights and practical tips, collectors can develop a more nuanced approach to building and maintaining a collection that captures the beauty and history of error coins.

5

Practical Collecting Guide

Error coin collecting is an engaging and rewarding hobby that attracts enthusiasts for its combination of historical intrigue, technical challenge, and the thrill of the hunt. This comprehensive guide provides beginners and intermediate collectors with the knowledge and tools necessary to excel in this niche of numismatics.

Step-by-Step Tutorials for Beginners and Intermediate Collectors

Embarking on the journey of collecting error coins is both exciting and demanding. This guide is designed to walk you through the foundational steps of building a robust error coin collection, from education to acquisition, and finally to the organization and preservation of your coins.

Starting Your Collection

1. **Educate Yourself:** Before you begin collecting, it's crucial to understand what error coins are and how they differ from normal issues. Resources such as numismatic books, online forums like CoinTalk, and memberships in numismatic clubs like the American Numismatic Association can provide invaluable information and connections.
2. **Set Collecting Goals:** Error coins come in a wide variety of types, each with its own appeal. Some collectors are fascinated by double dies, others by off-center strikes or wrong planchet errors. You might also find interest in focusing on errors from specific mints or historical periods. Setting clear goals helps in focusing your collecting efforts and resources.
3. **Establish a Budget:** The cost of error coins can range from a few dollars to thousands, depending on rarity and demand. It's important to set a realistic budget that aligns with your financial situation and collecting goals. This budget will guide your purchasing decisions and help prevent overspending.

Acquiring Error Coins

1. **Where to Find Error Coins:**

   - **Coin Shows:** Attending local or national coin shows can provide opportunities to meet dealers who specialize in error coins. These events allow you to view a wide variety of coins and learn from experienced collectors.
   - **Online Auctions and Forums:** Platforms like eBay and Heritage Auctions offer sections dedicated to error coins. These venues are excellent for finding deals but require a cautious approach to ensure authenticity.
   - **Local Coin Shops:** Develop relationships with local coin shop owners. Some may occasionally get error coins in stock, and building a rapport can lead to them contacting you when something interesting comes in.

2. **Assessing Coins:**

   - **Visual Inspection:** Learning to identify error coins involves understanding what to look for, such as misalignments, unusual markings, or differences in metal texture. A magnifying glass or a jeweler's loupe is essential for spotting these subtleties.

- **Handling Coins:** Always handle coins by their edges to avoid any damage from oils or dirt on your fingers. Cotton gloves are recommended when handling more valuable pieces to preserve their condition.

Organizing and Cataloging

1. **Cataloging Your Collection:** Keeping a detailed record of your collection is crucial. For each coin, record details like the type of error, acquisition date, purchase price, and any relevant historical or market information. Digital tools like Excel or specialized collection software can facilitate this process.
2. **Storing Coins:** Proper storage is key to maintaining the condition of your coins. Opt for acid-free holders, tubes, or albums to store your coins. These storage solutions should be kept in a climate-controlled environment to prevent damage from humidity and temperature fluctuations.

Enhancing Your Collecting Experience

1. **Join Collecting Forums:** Participating in online forums can enhance your knowledge and provide access to a community of like-minded enthusiasts. These platforms often offer insights into rare finds, trading opportunities, and personalized advice from seasoned collectors.
2. **Attend Workshops and Seminars:** Many numismatic clubs and associations host educational events that can greatly enhance your understanding of numismatics, including error coins. These are invaluable for making informed collecting decisions and networking with experts.
3. **Continuing Education:** The field of numismatics is ever-evolving, with new discoveries and research constantly changing what we know about error coins. Continuing your education through courses, books, and articles is essential to staying current in the hobby.

By following these detailed steps, beginners and intermediate collectors can not only start their collection of error coins but also develop a sophisticated approach to expanding and maintaining it. This systematic approach ensures that each collector not only enjoys the pursuit of new additions but also appreciates the broader historical and cultural significance of their collection.

Methods for Searching, Authenticating, and Preserving Error Coins

Navigating the world of error coins requires a strategic approach to searching, a keen eye for authentication, and meticulous care in preservation. This comprehensive guide delves into each of these aspects, providing both beginners and experienced collectors with the essential tools and knowledge to enhance their collecting endeavors.

Effective Searching Techniques

Regular Checking: One of the most straightforward methods for finding error coins is by regularly examining your own change and bank rolls. Coins in everyday circulation can sometimes reveal surprising treasures. An error coin might just pop up in your loose change from grocery shopping or among rolls of coins you can obtain from banks.

Networking: Engaging with numismatic clubs and online communities such as CoinTalk or the forums on Numista can be incredibly fruitful. These platforms allow collectors to share finds, sell trades, and provide alerts about error coins on the market. Networking can also lead to insider knowledge on private sales and auctions not generally available to the public.

Specialized Dealers and Shows: Attending coin shows and visiting specialized dealers can increase your chances of finding high-quality error coins. Dealers often have a deep understanding of their inventory, including the subtleties that make each error coin unique, and can offer pieces that are not available elsewhere.

Authenticating Error Coins

Understanding Authentication:

- **Visual Authentication:** Mastering the art of visually inspecting coins is crucial. This involves learning to identify discrepancies in mint marks, abnormal weights, and anomalies in the artwork that might indicate an error. For example, double dies will exhibit doubling in elements such as lettering or dates, which can be distinct from machine doubling.
- **Third-Party Grading Services:** Utilizing respected grading services such as the Professional Coin Grading Service (PCGS) or Numismatic Guaranty Corporation (NGC) can add a layer of authenticity to your coins. These organizations assess and encapsulate coins, providing a grade that is widely accepted by collectors and dealers alike, thereby enhancing the coin's value and tradeability.

Tools for Authentication:

- **Magnifying Glass or Loupe:** This is an essential tool for any collector. It allows for close examination of small details that are not visible to the naked eye.
- **Digital Scales:** Accurate scales are crucial for confirming that a coin's weight matches its official specifications, which is particularly important for identifying wrong planchet errors where the coin may be struck on a planchet intended for another denomination.

Preserving Your Collection

Proper Handling and Storage:

- **Handling:** Always handle coins by the edges to avoid contamination from oils and dirt on your fingers. Wearing gloves, preferably made of soft cotton or nitrile, can provide an additional layer of protection.
- **Storage Options:** Invest in high-quality storage solutions such as archival-quality flips, holders, or capsules. These materials ensure that the coin is protected from environmental factors and physical damage. It's critical to use products that are free from PVC, which can release harmful acids over time.

Environmental Considerations:

- **Humidity and Temperature:** Maintaining a controlled environment is essential for preserving the integrity of your coins. Excessive humidity can lead to corrosion, while fluctuating temperatures can cause condensation. Strive for a stable environment with low humidity and minimal temperature variation.
- **Security:** As your collection grows, so does its value and the need for secure storage. Investing in a high-quality safe or renting a safety deposit box at a bank can safeguard your valuable pieces against theft and damage.

By adhering to these detailed strategies for searching, authenticating, and preserving error coins, collectors can significantly enhance the quality and security of their collections. Regularly engaging in community networks and continuing education on authentication techniques will keep collectors informed of new opportunities and pitfalls in the field. Proper handling and storage will ensure that each coin's physical and historical value is maintained, making your collection a source of pride and historical reverence. Through diligent practice of these methods, collectors will not only enrich their own collecting experience but also contribute to the broader numismatic community by helping to preserve these fascinating pieces of monetary history.

Investment Advice and Market Trends

Investing in error coins is as much an art as it is a science. It requires not only an understanding of the numismatic significance of these coins but also an acute awareness of the market dynamics. Below are strategies and insights designed to guide both novice and seasoned collectors in navigating the complex landscape of error coin investment.

Understanding the Market

1. **Market Research:** Staying informed is crucial in the volatile market of numismatics. Subscriptions to leading numismatic publications such as "Coin World" or "Numismatic News" provide insights into market trends, auction results, and feature articles on rare finds and market analyses. Online databases and auction platforms like Heritage Auctions or Stack's Bowers offer real-time data on prices and demand, allowing collectors to track how similar coins are valued and traded in the market.
2. **Specialize:** Specializing in a specific type of error coin, such as double dies or off-center strikes, can significantly enhance your expertise and standing within the collecting community. This focus allows for deeper understanding of the nuances of these errors and better predictions of their market behaviors. Specialization also aids in building a network of fellow enthusiasts and experts who can provide leads on available coins and emerging trends.

Investment Strategies

1. **Long-term vs. Short-term:** Decide on your investment horizon. Some collectors invest in error coins for quick flips based on market trends, while others adopt a long-term perspective, holding onto coins that are likely to appreciate in value over years or even decades. Long-term investments tend to be more stable, benefiting from gradual market appreciation and reduced impact from short-term market volatility.

2. **Diversification:** While specializing can be beneficial, diversifying your collection across different types of error coins and other numismatic areas can mitigate risk. Market demand for certain types of errors may fluctuate, and having a diverse portfolio ensures that a dip in one segment won't drastically impact your overall collection's value.

Selling Your Coins

1. **Timing:** The timing of selling your coins can significantly impact their sale price. Monitor market trends closely and consider selling during peak demand for error coins or when a particular error becomes historically significant or popular among collectors. Keeping an eye on economic indicators can also provide clues on when collectors might be spending more freely on hobbies.
2. **Sales Venues:**

   - **Auctions:** Major auction houses often attract serious collectors and can therefore fetch higher prices for rare error coins. These venues are particularly effective for selling high-value or highly unique errors.
   - **Direct Sales:** Selling directly to other collectors or dealers can be more straightforward and may yield faster transactions. Leveraging relationships within numismatic clubs or online communities can facilitate these sales, often at better prices due to the reduced need for intermediary fees.

By integrating the above strategies with detailed tutorials on searching, authenticating, and preserving error coins, this guide aims to provide collectors with a robust toolkit for successful collecting and investing. From understanding the foundational aspects of each error coin to mastering the complexities of the market, collectors are equipped to make informed decisions. This comprehensive approach not only enhances the collector's ability to grow their collection but also protects and maximizes their investment in the dynamic field of numismatics.

Whether just beginning your journey into collecting error coins or looking to refine and expand an existing collection, the insights and strategies outlined here will help you navigate the intricacies of the market. Collectors are encouraged to remain adaptive and informed, continually evolving their strategies to align with both market conditions and personal collecting goals.

6

Mastering Numismatics Through Self-Assessment and Interactive Learning

In the fascinating world of coin collecting, continuous learning and skill enhancement are pivotal. This chapter is dedicated to providing coin collectors, especially those with a focus on error coins, with a structured approach to enhancing their numismatic expertise through self-assessment and interactive exercises. These hands-on activities are designed to deepen understanding of coin identification, valuation, and historical context—all crucial for becoming a proficient numismatist.

Developing Your Numismatic Eye

The ability to distinguish between normal coins and those with errors is a crucial skill for any numismatist. Developing this skill requires regular practice and a keen eye for detail. This section outlines practical exercises and methods to help collectors refine their error detection abilities.

Visual Comparison Challenges

Visual comparison is a fundamental technique for identifying coin errors. By comparing standard coins to those with errors, collectors can learn to recognize subtle differences and nuances. Here are some detailed steps and examples to guide you through this process:

Double Dies vs. Normal Strikes:

- **Double Dies:** Coins with double dies show a noticeable duplication of design elements, such as letters or numbers. This occurs when the die, used to strike the coin, has been impressed more than once, resulting in a doubled image.
- **Normal Strikes:** Standard coins, struck correctly, do not exhibit this doubling.

To practice, follow these steps:

1. **Gather High-Resolution Images:** Collect images of both double die and normal strike coins. Ensure the images are clear and detailed enough to see small features.
2. **Side-by-Side Comparison:** Place images of double die coins next to normal strike coins. Use a magnifying glass or digital zoom to closely examine the letters, numbers, and other design elements.
3. **Note the Differences:** Pay attention to the doubling in the double die coins. Compare the same elements on the normal strike coins to understand what a correctly struck coin should look like.

Off-center and Broadstrikes:

- **Off-center Strikes:** These coins are struck outside the intended area, causing part of the design to be missing or off-center.
- **Broadstrikes:** These occur when a coin is struck without the collar that normally shapes the edges, resulting in a coin that is broader and thinner than usual.

Steps to practice:

1. **Collect Examples:** Obtain images or actual coins of both off-center and broadstrikes, alongside their correctly struck counterparts.

2. **Detailed Examination:** Compare the misaligned designs of off-center strikes and the expanded surfaces of broadstrikes to the standard coins.
3. **Identify Characteristics:** Look for specific markers, such as the missing parts of the design in off-center strikes and the lack of a defined edge in broadstrikes.

By consistently practicing these visual comparison challenges, collectors can train their eyes to quickly and accurately spot errors in coins.

Error Identification Drills

To enhance error identification skills, creating and engaging in structured drills can be highly effective. These drills should be designed to cover a wide range of error types and provide immediate feedback to reinforce learning.

Setting Up Error Identification Drills:

1. **Compile a List of Error Types:** Begin by listing various error types, such as clipped planchets, cuds, die cracks, and misstrikes. Include a brief description and characteristics of each error type.

   - **Clipped Planchets:** Coins that have a portion missing due to irregular cutting of the blank.
   - **Cuds:** Raised areas on the coin where a piece of the die has broken off.
   - **Die Cracks:** Thin, raised lines on the coin caused by cracks in the die.
   - **Misstrikes:** Coins that are not properly aligned or struck multiple times.

2. **Create Multiple-Choice Questions:** For each error type, prepare multiple-choice questions that include close-up images of coins. The questions should challenge collectors to identify the type of error depicted.

   - **Example Question:** Look at the image below. What type of error is shown on this coin? a. Clipped Planchet b. Die Crack c. Cud d. Broadstrike

3. **Interactive Quizzes:** Use online tools or printable formats to create interactive quizzes. These quizzes should allow for immediate feedback, so collectors can learn from their mistakes and understand why a particular answer is correct.

Periodic Review and Practice:

   - **Regular Drills:** Set aside time regularly to go through these identification drills. Repetition is key to reinforcing knowledge and improving identification speed.
   - **Update with New Examples:** Continuously update your drills with new examples and variations of errors to keep the practice challenging and comprehensive.

Advanced Identification Techniques:

   - **Magnification Tools:** Use magnifying glasses, loupes, or digital microscopes to examine coins closely. High magnification can reveal details that are not visible to the naked eye, such as fine die cracks or subtle doubling.

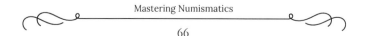

- **Lighting Conditions:** Experiment with different lighting conditions to see how light affects the visibility of certain errors. Oblique lighting, where light is shone at an angle, can highlight raised or recessed areas on the coin surface.

Case Studies:

- **Detailed Analysis of Famous Errors:** Study well-documented cases of famous error coins. Analyze what made these errors significant and how they were identified. Understanding these cases can provide deeper insights into error detection and valuation.
- **Historical Context:** Place errors within their historical context to understand why they occurred. For example, during periods of high coin production, such as wartime, certain errors may have been more prevalent due to rushed production processes.

By engaging in visual comparison challenges and structured error identification drills, collectors can develop a sharp eye for detail and a thorough understanding of various coin errors. This section provides the foundational exercises needed to enhance your numismatic skills, making you a more proficient and knowledgeable collector. Regular practice, combined with the use of advanced tools and continuous learning, will ensure that you can quickly and accurately identify errors, adding value and depth to your coin collection.

Enhancing Valuation Skills with Simulations (500 words)

Understanding the valuation of error coins is crucial for making informed buying and selling decisions. By simulating real-world scenarios and engaging in practical exercises, collectors can enhance their skills in determining the market value of coins. This section outlines how to use market analysis simulations and practical valuation exercises to build a deeper understanding of coin pricing dynamics.

Market Analysis Simulation

Simulating an auction setting allows collectors to experience the dynamics of coin auctions and sales without financial risk. This practice helps in understanding how various factors influence coin values and improves decision-making skills.

Mock Auction:

- **Creating Scenarios:** Develop scenarios with detailed descriptions of various coins. Include information on each coin's condition, rarity, and historical significance. For example, describe a rare 1955 doubled die Lincoln cent in excellent condition versus one in fair condition.
- **Budgeting:** Assign a fictional budget to participants. This helps in practicing how to allocate funds wisely during an auction.
- **Bidding Process:** Conduct the mock auction by having participants bid on the coins based on their assigned budgets. This exercise helps participants understand how competition and perceived value affect bidding strategies.

Price Estimation Game:

- **Description-Based Valuation:** Provide descriptions or images of various coins without revealing their market prices. Ask participants to estimate the value of each coin based on factors like rarity, demand, and historical value.
- **Revealing Actual Prices:** After the estimates are made, reveal the actual market prices. Discuss the differences between the estimated and actual values to understand how different attributes influence pricing.

By participating in these simulations, collectors can gain practical experience in auction settings and develop a better understanding of the factors that influence coin values.

Practical Valuation Exercises

Engaging in practical valuation exercises enhances the ability to conduct market analyses and understand how external factors impact coin prices.

Comparative Market Analysis:

- **Hypothetical Profiles:** Create profiles of various error coins, including details on their condition, rarity, and historical context. For example, compare a 1972 Lincoln cent with a doubled die obverse in different grades (e.g., MS-65 vs. MS-60).
- **Analyzing Market Trends:** Use historical data to analyze how similar coins have been priced in different market conditions. This helps in understanding the impact of factors such as economic climate and collector interest on coin values.

Step-by-Step Guide:

1. **Research:** Start by researching the current market prices of coins similar to those in the hypothetical profiles. Use online auction sites, coin price guides, and recent sales data.
2. **Condition Assessment:** Evaluate how the condition of each coin affects its value. Higher grades typically command higher prices.
3. **Rarity and Demand:** Consider how the rarity and demand for each coin influence its market price. Rare coins in high demand are usually more valuable.
4. **Historical Significance:** Assess the historical context and its impact on the coin's value. Coins with significant historical backgrounds often hold higher value.

Discussion and Analysis:

- **Comparing Results:** After completing the analysis, compare your valuations with actual market data. Discuss any discrepancies and the reasons behind them.
- **Learning from Trends:** Identify trends and patterns in the data. For example, how do economic downturns or booms affect coin prices? How does collector interest shift over time?

By consistently practicing these valuation exercises, collectors can build a solid foundation in understanding the intricacies of coin pricing. This knowledge not only enhances buying and selling decisions but also deepens the overall appreciation of numismatics. Through these simulations and exercises, collectors become more adept at navigating the market, ensuring that their collections are both valuable and historically significant.

Building a Historical Context Repository

Historical Significance Exercises

Understanding the historical context of coins can significantly enhance their value and your appreciation for them. Here are some exercises to help connect your collection to history:

Timeline Creation:

- **Research and Mapping**: For each coin in your collection, research key historical events that occurred during its minting period. Create a timeline that highlights these events and shows how they might have influenced the coin's design and any errors. For example, if you have a coin from 1943, you might note that it was produced during World War II, which led to changes in materials and minting processes.
- **Visual Representation**: Use digital tools like timeline software or physical charts to map out these timelines. This visual representation helps to contextualize your collection within broader historical narratives, making each coin a part of a larger story.

Fact-Checking Missions:

- **Verifying Historical Facts**: Regularly verify historical facts and claims about coins in your collection. Use reputable sources such as historical texts, academic journals, and trusted online databases to confirm the authenticity of the stories associated with your coins. For instance, if a coin is said to be rare due to a minting error during a specific historical event, check multiple sources to validate this information.
- **Documentation**: Keep detailed notes on your findings, including sources and any discrepancies you encounter. This not only reinforces the accuracy of your numismatic knowledge but also creates a reliable reference for future research.

By engaging in these historical significance exercises, collectors can deepen their understanding of the historical context of their coins, thereby enhancing the overall value and enjoyment of their collection.

Implementing Feedback Loops

Reflective Learning

Effective learning in numismatics involves continuous reflection on your experiences and findings. Here are some strategies to incorporate reflective learning into your collecting practices:

Journaling Techniques:

- **Detailed Journal:** Keep a detailed journal of your numismatic journey, noting new learnings, mistakes, and observations. This journal can include entries on why you acquired certain coins, the historical research you conducted, and insights gained from examining errors.
- **Progress Tracking:** Use the journal to track your progress over time. Regularly review past entries to see how your knowledge and skills have evolved. This reflection can help identify areas for further improvement and reinforce successful strategies.

Peer Review Sessions:

- **Engaging with Collectors:** Engage with other collectors through online forums, local clubs, or social media groups to share and discuss your findings. Present your collection and the historical research you've conducted for feedback.
- **Constructive Feedback:** Seek constructive feedback from peers to gain new insights and validate your assessments. Peers can offer different perspectives, point out overlooked details, and provide advice on improving your collection and research methods.

By incorporating these reflective learning techniques, collectors can continuously enhance their numismatic skills and knowledge. Journaling and peer review not only provide opportunities for self-assessment but also foster a sense of community and shared learning within the numismatic world.

By actively participating in these structured self-assessment and interactive learning activities, collectors can significantly enhance their numismatic skills. This chapter not only equips you with the tools to improve your coin collecting abilities but also encourages a deeper appreciation of the hobby through a methodical approach to learning and discovery. Whether you are a novice or an experienced collector, these exercises offer valuable opportunities to engage with your collection in a meaningful way, ensuring a rewarding and enduring numismatic journey.

7

Comprehensive
Reference Section

High-Quality Images, Descriptions, Rarity Scales, and Current Market Values

A detailed understanding of U.S. error coins is greatly enhanced by high-quality images, comprehensive descriptions, rarity scales, and current market values. This section aims to provide collectors with the tools they need to accurately identify and assess the value of their error coins.

High-Quality Images

Visual documentation is crucial for identifying error coins. High-resolution images allow collectors to see the fine details and nuances that differentiate error coins from standard issues. Here are some examples of how high-quality images can aid in identification:

1. 1955 Doubled Die Lincoln Cent:

- **Image Details:** Clear images showing the pronounced doubling of the date and inscriptions. Highlight the doubling in "LIBERTY" and "IN GOD WE TRUST."
- **Use of Lighting:** Employ angled lighting to accentuate the doubling effect, making it visible even in smaller details.

2. 2004-D Extra Leaf Wisconsin State Quarter:

- **Image Details:** Provide images of both high and low leaf varieties. Close-ups of the corn stalk showing the extra leaf detail.
- **Comparison:** Side-by-side images of the standard quarter and the error coin to illustrate the differences.

Comprehensive Descriptions

Descriptions are essential for understanding the specific characteristics of each error coin. Detailed descriptions help collectors know what to look for and provide context for the errors.

1. 1968 No S Proof Roosevelt Dime:

- **Description:** This proof dime was minted without the "S" mintmark, which is supposed to denote the San Francisco Mint. The absence of the mintmark is due to a minting error where a proof die was inadvertently used without the mintmark.
- **Identifying Features:** Proof finish, mirror-like surfaces, and the lack of the "S" mintmark.

2. 1972-D No FG Kennedy Half Dollar:

- **Description:** This error coin is missing the designer Frank Gasparro's initials ("FG") on the reverse. The error is typically due to over-polishing of the die, which removed the initials.
- **Identifying Features:** Absence of "FG" below the eagle's tail feathers and near the bottom of the shield.

Rarity Scales

Rarity scales help collectors understand the scarcity of their coins. The Sheldon Rarity Scale is commonly used, ranging from R-1 (common) to R-8 (unique).

1. 1955 Doubled Die Lincoln Cent:

- **Rarity:** R-4 (Very Scarce). This classification indicates that the coin is uncommon but not extremely rare.
- **Factors Affecting Rarity:** The number of coins struck with this error and how many have survived in various conditions.

2. 2000-P Sacagawea Dollar Mule with State Quarter Obverse:

- Rarity: R-7 (Extremely Rare). This classification denotes a very high level of scarcity.
- Factors Affecting Rarity: Limited number of known examples and the significant minting error.

Current Market Values

Market values for error coins fluctuate based on demand, condition, and rarity. Providing current market values helps collectors make informed buying, selling, or trading decisions.

1. 1982 No P Roosevelt Dime:

- **Value Range:** $50 to $300. Coins in higher grades with clear surfaces and strong strike command higher prices.
- **Factors Influencing Value:** Overall condition, clarity of the error, and market demand at the time of sale.

2. 1964 Kennedy Half Dollar Doubled Die Obverse:

- **Value Range:** $50 to $1,000. Coins with more pronounced doubling and higher grades fetch premium prices.
- **Factors Influencing Value:** Doubling clarity, coin condition, and collector interest.

Case Studies with Detailed Examples

1. 1955 Doubled Die Lincoln Cent

- **High-Quality Images:** Detailed close-ups of the date and inscriptions, showing the pronounced doubling effect.
- **Comprehensive Description:** This coin is one of the most famous doubled die errors. The doubling on the date and lettering is due to a misalignment during the die-making process, causing a second impression that did not align perfectly with the first.
- **Rarity Scale:** Rated as R-4 (Very Scarce), indicating its uncommon nature but with enough examples to make it collectible.
- **Current Market Values:** Prices vary significantly based on condition. Lower grade examples can sell for a few hundred dollars, while high-grade specimens in MS-65 condition or better can reach over $20,000.

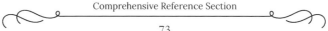

2. 2004-D Extra Leaf Wisconsin State Quarter

- **High-Quality Images:** Clear, high-resolution images showing both the high leaf and low leaf varieties. Highlight the extra leaf on the corn stalk.
- **Comprehensive Description:** This error occurred due to a die gouge that added an extra leaf to the corn stalk on the reverse side of the Wisconsin state quarter. There are two main varieties: high leaf and low leaf.
- **Rarity Scale:** Both varieties are considered scarce, with the high leaf being more valuable due to its greater rarity.
- **Current Market Values:** Values range from $50 to $1,500 depending on the variety and the coin's condition. High-grade examples of the high leaf variety can fetch the higher end of the price range.

3. 1968 No S Proof Roosevelt Dime

- **High-Quality Images:** Detailed images showing the absence of the "S" mintmark. Use lighting to highlight the proof finish and the error.
- **Comprehensive Description:** The 1968 proof Roosevelt dime was intended to bear an "S" mintmark for the San Francisco Mint, but due to a minting error, some were struck without the mintmark. These proof coins are highly sought after by collectors.
- **Rarity Scale:** Rated as R-7 (Extremely Rare), indicating a very limited number of these coins were produced and are available.
- **Current Market Values:** Extremely rare, these coins are valued between $15,000 and $25,000. Their value is driven by their rarity and the desirability of proof error coins.

4. 1982 No P Roosevelt Dime

- **High-Quality Images:** Close-up images showing the area where the "P" mintmark should be. Highlight the coin's overall condition.
- **Comprehensive Description:** This error coin lacks the "P" mintmark, which was introduced on Philadelphia-minted dimes in 1980. The error occurred because the mintmark was inadvertently left off the die.
- **Rarity Scale:** Considered relatively common among error coins, this is rated as R-3 (Scarce).
- **Current Market Values:** Values range from $50 for circulated examples to $300 for mint state coins. The price is influenced by the coin's condition and the visibility of the error.

5. 2000-P Sacagawea Dollar Mule with State Quarter Obverse

- **High-Quality Images:** Detailed images showing the mismatched obverse and reverse designs. Highlight the state quarter obverse paired with the Sacagawea dollar reverse.
- **Comprehensive Description:** One of the most famous modern mint errors, this coin features the obverse of a state quarter paired with the reverse of a Sacagawea dollar. This rare mule error is a result of a mix-up at the mint.
- **Rarity Scale:** Rated as R-7 (Extremely Rare), indicating very few examples are known to exist.
- **Current Market Values:** Extremely rare and highly valued, these coins range from $50,000 to $100,000. The coin's rarity and the significant error make it one of the most sought-after pieces in modern numismatics.

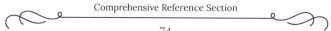

Practical Tips for Using This Section

- **Identifying Errors:** Use the high-quality images and descriptions to match your coins with known errors. Pay attention to the specific details and characteristics outlined in the descriptions.
- **Evaluating Condition:** Consider the coin's condition as described in the valuation examples. Coins in better condition will typically be more valuable.
- **Understanding Market Dynamics:** Keep an eye on current market trends and values. Error coins can fluctuate in value based on collector interest and market conditions.
- **Using Rarity Scales:** Apply the rarity scales to gauge how common or rare your coins are. This can help in determining their desirability and market value.

By leveraging the high-quality images, detailed descriptions, rarity scales, and current market values provided in this section, collectors can gain a comprehensive understanding of U.S. error coins. This knowledge empowers them to make informed decisions about their collections, enhancing their appreciation for the historical and numismatic significance of these fascinating coins.

Glossary of Numismatic Terms

A solid understanding of numismatic terminology is essential for any coin collector, particularly those interested in error coins. This glossary provides clear definitions of key terms used in numismatics, helping collectors to navigate the field with confidence and accuracy.

A

- **Abrasions:** Minor surface marks or scratches on a coin that can affect its grade.
- **Adjustment Marks:** Small, parallel scratches found on early U.S. coins caused by filing down overweight planchets to the correct weight before striking.
- **Alloy:** A mixture of two or more metals. Coins are often made from alloys to enhance durability.
- **Annealing:** The process of heating metal and then slowly cooling it to remove internal stresses, making it easier to strike.

B

- **Bag Marks:** Small marks or nicks on coins, typically from contact with other coins in a mint bag.
- **Base Metal:** Non-precious metal used to make coins, such as copper or nickel.
- **Beading:** Small, raised dots near the edge of a coin, often used as a border decoration.
- **Blank (Planchet):** The metal disc that is struck to create a coin.

C

- **Cameo:** A coin, usually a proof, with a frosted design that contrasts with a mirrored field.
- **Carbon Spot:** A dark spot on a coin, often caused by a small impurity in the metal.
- **Cartwheel Effect:** The distinctive pattern of light reflected from a coin's surface, especially on uncirculated coins.

- **Clad Coin:** A coin composed of layers of different metals bonded together. U.S. dimes, quarters, and half dollars made after 1964 are clad coins.
- **Clipping:** The illegal practice of shaving metal from the edges of coins.
- **Collar:** A metal ring used in coin production to hold the planchet in place during striking, which also forms the coin's edge.

D

- **Debasement:** The reduction in the precious metal content of a coin.
- **Denomination:** The face value of a coin.
- **Device:** The principal design element on a coin, such as a portrait or emblem.
- **Die:** A metal piece engraved with a design used to strike one side of a coin.
- **Die Crack:** A raised line on a coin caused by a crack in the die used to strike the coin.
- **Doubled Die:** A die that has been struck more than once during its creation, resulting in a coin with doubled design elements.

E

- **Edge:** The side of a coin, which may be plain, reeded, lettered, or decorated.
- **Encapsulated Coin:** A coin that has been graded, authenticated, and sealed in a protective plastic holder by a third-party grading service.
- **Engraver:** The artist who creates the designs and models for coins.
- **Error Coin:** A coin that exhibits a mistake or anomaly from the minting process, such as a misstrike or doubling.

F

- **Face Value:** The nominal value of a coin as stated by the issuing authority.
- **Field:** The flat background area of a coin, free of design elements.
- **Flan:** Another term for a blank or planchet, the metal disc used to strike a coin.
- **Frosting:** The matte finish applied to certain parts of a coin's design, typically seen on proof coins.

G

- **Grade:** The condition of a coin, typically determined by a professional grading service and expressed in terms such as Good (G), Very Fine (VF), or Mint State (MS).
- **Grading Service:** An independent company that evaluates a coin's condition, assigns it a grade, and encapsulates it in a protective holder.

H

- **Hairlines:** Fine scratches on a coin's surface, often from cleaning or handling.
- **Hub:** A positive impression of a coin's design used to create dies.

I

- **Incuse:** A design element that is impressed into the surface of a coin, rather than raised.
- **Ingot:** A bar of metal, typically of a precious metal, cast in a standardized shape for storage or manufacturing.

L

- **Lamination:** A defect in a coin caused by impurities or internal stresses that result in a piece of metal separating from the coin's surface.
- **Legend:** The inscription on a coin, often stating the country of issue or a motto.

M

- **Matte Finish:** A dull or non-reflective surface finish applied to some proof coins.
- **Medal Alignment:** When a coin's obverse and reverse are aligned such that the top of the obverse matches the top of the reverse, opposite of coin alignment.
- **Mint:** A facility where coins are produced.
- **Mint Mark:** A small letter or symbol on a coin that indicates the mint where it was produced.
- **Mule:** A coin struck with obverse and reverse dies not intended to be used together, often from different coin series.

N

- **Numismatics:** The study or collection of coins, paper money, and medals.
- **Numismatist:** A person who studies or collects coins, paper money, and medals.

O

- **Obverse:** The front side of a coin, typically featuring the main design or portrait.

P

- **Patina:** The surface coloration or tone of a coin caused by age, oxidation, or chemical treatment.
- **Planchet:** The metal disc that is struck to create a coin, also known as a blank.
- **Proof:** A specially made coin struck with extra care, typically for collectors, featuring a high-quality finish and often multiple strikes.

R

- **Reeding:** The series of grooves or serrations on the edge of a coin.
- **Relief:** The raised design elements on a coin's surface.
- **Restrike:** A coin that is struck later than its original issue date, often with original dies.
- **Reverse:** The back side of a coin, usually displaying secondary designs or inscriptions.

S

- **Sheldon Scale:** A 70-point scale used to grade the condition of coins, with 1 being Poor and 70 being Mint State perfection.
- **Strike:** The process of stamping a design onto a planchet to create a coin.

T

- **Toning:** The natural coloration or patina that forms on a coin over time due to chemical reactions with the environment.
- **Type Set:** A collection of coins that includes one example of each type or major design issued within a series.

W

- **Wear:** The loss of detail on a coin due to circulation or handling.
- **Whizzing:** The process of polishing a coin with a wire brush or other mechanical means to simulate luster, often considered a deceptive practice.

Conclusion

As we reach the final pages of our journey through the fascinating world of U.S. error coins, it's a good moment to pause and reflect on the depth and richness of what we've explored together. This book, which we might aptly call the "Coin Collecting Bible," has aimed to provide a holistic view of numismatics—blending historical narratives, technical insights, and practical advice to create a comprehensive guide for collectors at all levels.

The Minting Process: Foundation of Understanding

Let's start with the basics. We've spent quite a bit of time unpacking the minting process. Understanding how coins are made is the cornerstone of appreciating how errors occur. The journey from raw metal to finished coin involves numerous steps—each a potential point for something to go awry. By grasping the intricacies of planchet preparation, die creation, and the striking process, you gain a deeper connection to your collection. Each error coin isn't just a minting mishap; it's a piece of art, a snippet of history captured in metal. This foundational knowledge transforms the way we look at these coins, allowing us to see the beauty in their imperfections.

The Unique Allure of Error Coins

Error coins have a unique allure that goes beyond their market value. They are anomalies, results of momentary lapses in a highly controlled environment, and each one tells a story. Whether it's a doubled die, a misstruck planchet, or a coin missing a crucial detail, these errors make each piece distinctive. Collectors are drawn to these quirks because they embody the unpredictability of the minting process. In a world where precision is the norm, these errors remind us of the human element involved in coin production. They are tangible proof that even in the most precise systems, there's room for the unexpected.

The Stories Behind the Coins

One of the most engaging parts of this book has been the stories behind specific error coins. Take the 1955 Doubled Die Lincoln Cent or the 2004-D Extra Leaf Wisconsin State Quarter. Each of these coins has a backstory that adds layers of interest and value. We've explored how historical events, technological shifts, and sheer happenstance have led to the creation of these errors. These narratives turn each coin into a piece of living history. They are not just artifacts but storytellers, each with a tale of its own, linking us to moments and decisions from the past.

Insights from Experts

Gaining insights from experts in the field has been another cornerstone of this book. Interviews with seasoned numismatists, mint employees, and collectors have provided a wealth of knowledge that's hard to come by. Their experiences and advice on identifying, authenticating, and valuing error coins are invaluable. It's like having a personal mentor guiding you through the nuances of the hobby. These expert perspectives add depth to your understanding and help you become more proficient in recognizing and appreciating the subtle details that make each coin unique.

Practical Guidance for Collectors

Whether you're just starting or have been collecting for years, practical advice is crucial. This book has aimed to be a hands-on guide, offering step-by-step tutorials for searching, authenticating, and preserving error coins. We've discussed how to set up and maintain your collection, from choosing the right storage solutions to keeping detailed records. These practical tips ensure that your collection remains organized and well-preserved, enhancing its value and your enjoyment.

Embracing Modern Technology

In today's digital age, technology plays an increasingly significant role in numismatics. The chapter on interactive and multimedia content highlighted how tools like augmented reality (AR) and companion websites can enhance your collecting experience. Imagine pointing your phone at a coin and instantly accessing detailed information and 3D models. These technologies make learning about and appreciating coins more interactive and engaging. Embracing these innovations ensures that the hobby remains relevant and exciting, opening new avenues for exploration and education.

Comprehensive Reference Materials

A significant part of this book is dedicated to serving as a comprehensive reference guide. Detailed catalogs of U.S. error coins by denomination, complete with high-quality images, descriptions, rarity scales, and current market values, provide an invaluable resource. This section allows you to quickly identify and assess the value of your coins, making informed decisions about your collection. The glossary of numismatic terms and detailed index further enhance the usability of the book, making it easy to navigate and find specific information.

Documenting and Cataloging Your Collection

Effective documentation and cataloging are key to managing a coin collection. We've discussed how to create a digital catalog, including the essential information to record about each coin. Best practices for organizing and maintaining your collection ensure that it remains systematic and accessible. Detailed records help you track the history and value of your coins, adding another layer of enjoyment and professionalism to your hobby.

Looking to the Future: Trends in Numismatics

The world of coin collecting is always evolving, and staying ahead means keeping up with emerging trends and technologies. We've explored how blockchain technology, artificial intelligence (AI), and machine learning are set to revolutionize the field. Blockchain can provide secure and transparent ways to authenticate and track the provenance of coins, while AI and machine learning can enhance error detection and coin grading. Understanding and adopting these technologies will help you stay at the forefront of numismatics.

Staying Ahead in the Market

The market for error coins can be dynamic and sometimes unpredictable. Staying informed about market trends and being adaptable to new technologies are crucial for success. This book has provided strategies for leveraging modern tools and keeping up with trends, ensuring that you can make informed decisions and maximize the potential of your collection. Embracing change and continuously educating yourself are keys to staying ahead in this evolving market.

Celebrating the Art and Science of Coin Collecting

Ultimately, this book is a celebration of the art and science of coin collecting. It honors the rich history and intricate craftsmanship that go into each coin, while also embracing the future of the hobby. Whether you are a seasoned collector or a curious newcomer, this book aims to inspire and equip you with the knowledge and tools needed to explore the fascinating world of U.S. error coins.

Final Reflections

As you continue your numismatic journey, remember that each coin in your collection is more than just a piece of metal. It's a piece of history, a work of art, and a testament to the human element within the minting process. Collecting coins is not just about amassing valuable items; it's about appreciating the stories and craftsmanship behind each piece. This book has aimed to provide a comprehensive guide to understanding, collecting, and valuing error coins, enriching your appreciation for this rewarding hobby.

The world of coin collecting is vast and ever-evolving. Stay curious, stay informed, and most importantly, enjoy the journey. The "Coin Collecting Bible" is not just a book; it's a companion that will guide you through the fascinating realms of numismatics, helping you build a collection that is both meaningful and valuable.

Thank you for embarking on this journey with us. Happy collecting!

Bonus

Please scan this QR Code to access the bonus contents of :
The Comprehensive US Error Coins Handbook:

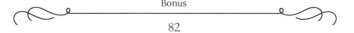

Made in the USA
Columbia, SC
01 March 2025